The Productive Programmer

Neal Ford
foreword by David Bock

O'REILLY®

Beijing · Cambridge · Farnham · Köln · Sebastopol · Taipei · Tokyo

The Productive Programmer
by Neal Ford

Copyright © 2008 Neal Ford. All rights reserved.
Printed in the United States of America.

Published by O'Reilly Media, Inc., 1005 Gravenstein Highway North, Sebastopol, CA 95472.

O'Reilly books may be purchased for educational, business, or sales promotional use. Online editions are also available for most titles (*http://safari.oreilly.com*). For more information, contact our corporate/institutional sales department: (800) 998-9938 or *corporate@oreilly.com*.

Editor:	Mike Loukides	**Indexer:**	Fred Brown
Production Editor:	Loranah Dimant	**Cover Designer:**	Mark Paglietti
Copyeditor:	Emily Quill	**Interior Designer:**	David Futato
Proofreader:	Loranah Dimant	**Illustrator:**	Robert Romano
		Photographer:	Candy Ford

Printing History:

    July 2008:   First Edition.

This book uses RepKover™, a durable and flexible lay-flat binding.

ISBN: 978-0-596-51978-0

[C]

1213988486

CONTENTS

FOREWORD   vii

PREFACE   ix

1 INTRODUCTION   1
       Why a Book on Programmer Productivity?   2
       What This Book Is About   3
       Where to Go Now?   5

Part One   MECHANICS
_____

2 ACCELERATION   9
       Launching Pad   10
       Accelerators   18
       Macros   33
       Summary   35

3 FOCUS   37
       Kill Distractions   38
       Search Trumps Navigation   40
       Find Hard Targets   42
       Use Rooted Views   44
       Use Sticky Attributes   46
       Use Project-Based Shortcuts   47
       Multiply Your Monitors   48
       Segregate Your Workspace with Virtual Desktops   48
       Summary   50

4 AUTOMATION   51
       Don't Reinvent Wheels   53
       Cache Stuff Locally   53
       Automate Your Interaction with Web Sites   54
       Interact with RSS Feeds   54
       Subvert Ant for Non-Build Tasks   56
       Subvert Rake for Common Tasks   57
       Subvert Selenium to Walk Web Pages   58
       Use Bash to Harvest Exception Counts   60
       Replace Batch Files with Windows Power Shell   61
       Use Mac OS X Automator to Delete Old Downloads   62
       Tame Command-Line Subversion   62
       Build a SQL Splitter in Ruby   64
       Justifying Automation   65

	Don't Shave Yaks	67
	Summary	68
5	CANONICALITY	69
	DRY Version Control	70
	Use a Canonical Build Machine	72
	Indirection	73
	Use Virtualization	80
	DRY Impedance Mismatches	80
	DRY Documentation	88
	Summary	93

Part Two PRACTICE

6	TEST-DRIVEN DESIGN	97
	Evolving Tests	99
	Code Coverage	105
7	STATIC ANALYSIS	109
	Byte Code Analysis	110
	Source Analysis	112
	Generate Metrics with Panopticode	113
	Analysis for Dynamic Languages	116
8	GOOD CITIZENSHIP	119
	Breaking Encapsulation	120
	Constructors	121
	Static Methods	121
	Criminal Behavior	126
9	YAGNI	129
10	ANCIENT PHILOSOPHERS	135
	Aristotle's Essential and Accidental Properties	136
	Occam's Razor	137
	The Law of Demeter	140
	Software Lore	141
11	QUESTION AUTHORITY	143
	Angry Monkeys	144
	Fluent Interfaces	145
	Anti-Objects	147
12	META-PROGRAMMING	149
	Java and Reflection	150
	Testing Java with Groovy	151
	Writing Fluent Interfaces	152
	Whither Meta-Programming?	154
13	COMPOSED METHOD AND SLAP	155
	Composed Method in Action	156

    SLAP   160

14   POLYGLOT PROGRAMMING   165
    How Did We Get Here? And Where Exactly Is Here?   166
    Where Are We Going? And How Do We Get There?   169
    Ola's Pyramid   173

15   FIND THE PERFECT TOOLS   175
    The Quest for the Perfect Editor   176
    The Candidates   179
    Choosing the Right Tool for the Job   180
    Un-Choosing the Wrong Tools   186

16   CONCLUSION: CARRYING ON THE CONVERSATION   189

    APPENDIX: BUILDING BLOCKS   191

    INDEX   199

FOREWORD

The individual productivity of programmers varies widely in our industry. What most of us might be able to get done in a week, some are able to get done in a day. Why is that? The short answer concerns mastery of the tools developers have at their disposal. The long answer is about the real *awareness* of the tools' capabilities and mastery of the thought process for using them. The truth lies somewhere between a methodology and a philosophy, and that is what Neal captures in this book.

The seeds of this book were planted in the fall of 2005, on a ride back to the airport. Neal asked me, "Do you think the world needs another book on regular expressions?" From there, the conversation turned to topics of books we wished existed. I thought back to a point in my career where I feel I made the leap from merely good to very productive, and how and why that happened. I said, "I don't know what the title of the book is, but the subtitle would be 'using the command line as an integrated development environment.'" At the time I credited my increased productivity to the acceleration I experienced using the bash shell, but it was more than that—it was my increasing familiarity with that tool as I stopped having to struggle to do things and could just get them done. We spent some time discussing that hyperproductivity and how to bottle it. Several years, untold conversations, and a series of lectures later, Neal has produced a definitive work on the subject.

In his book *Programming Perl* (O'Reilly), Larry Wall describes the three virtues of a programmer as "laziness, impatience, and hubris." Laziness, because you will expend effort to reduce the amount of overall work necessary. Impatience, because it will anger you if you are wasting time doing something the computer could do faster for you. And hubris, because excessive pride will make you write programs that other people won't say bad things about. This book doesn't use any of those words (and I used *grep* to check), but as you read on, you will find this sentiment echoed and expanded in this content.

There are several books that have had a great influence on my career, changing the way I see the world. I wish I had this book in hand 10 years ago; I'm sure it will have a profound influence on those who read it.

—David Bock
Principal Consultant
CodeSherpas

PREFACE

Many years ago, I taught training classes for experienced developers who were learning new technologies (like Java). The disparity between the productivity of the students always struck me: some were orders of magnitude more effective. And I don't mean in the tool they were using: I mean in their general interaction with the computer. I used to make a joke to a few of my colleagues that some of the people in the class weren't running their computers, they were walking them. Following a logical conclusion, that made me question my own productivity. Am I getting the most efficient use out of the computer I'm running (or walking)?

Fast-forward years later, and David Bock and I got into a conversation about this very thing. Many of our younger coworkers never really used command-line tools, and didn't understand how they could possibly offer more productivity than the elaborate IDEs of today. As David recounts in the foreword to this book, we chatted about this and decided to write a book about using the command line more effectively. We contacted a publisher, and started gathering all the command-line voodoo we could find from friends and coworkers.

Then, several things happened. David started his own consulting company, and he and his wife had their first children: triplets! Well, David now clearly has more on his hands than he can handle. At the same time, I was coming to the conclusion that a book purely about command-line tricks would be perhaps the most boring book ever written. At about that time, I was working on a project in Bangalore, and my pair-programmer partner, Mujir, was talking about code patterns and how to identify them. It hit me like a ton of bricks. I had been seeing patterns in all the recipes I'd been gathering. Instead of a massive collection of command-line tricks, the conversation should be about *identifying* what makes developers more productive. That's what you hold in your hands right now.

Who This Book Is For

This isn't a book for end users who want to use their computers more effectively. It's a book about *programmer* productivity, which means I can make a lot of assumptions about the audience. Developers are the ultimate power users, so I don't spend a lot of time on basic stuff. A tech-savvy user should certainly learn something (especially in Part I), but the target remains developers.

There is no explicit order to this book, so feel free to wander around as you like or read it front to back. The only connections between the topics appear in unexpected ways, so reading it front to back may have a slight advantage, but not enough to suggest that's the only way to consume this book.

Conventions Used in This Book

The following typographical conventions are used in this book:

Italic

  Indicates new terms, URLs, email addresses, filenames, and file extensions.

`Constant width`

  Used for program listings, as well as within paragraphs to refer to program elements such as variable or function names, databases, data types, environment variables, statements, and keywords.

`Constant width bold`

  Shows commands or other text that should be typed literally by the user.

`Constant width italic`

  Shows text that should be replaced with user-supplied values or by values determined by context.

Using Code Examples

This book is here to help you get your job done. In general, you may use the code in this book in your programs and documentation. You do not need to contact us for permission unless you're reproducing a significant portion of the code. For example, writing a program that uses several chunks of code from this book does not require permission. Selling or distributing a CD-ROM of examples from O'Reilly books does require permission. Answering a question by citing this book and quoting example code does not require permission. Incorporating a significant amount of example code from this book into your product's documentation does require permission.

We appreciate, but do not require, attribution. An attribution usually includes the title, author, publisher, and ISBN. For example: "*The Productive Programmer* by Neal Ford. Copyright 2008 Neal Ford, 978-0-596-51978-0."

If you feel your use of code examples falls outside fair use or the permission given above, feel free to contact us at *permissions@oreilly.com*.

How to Contact Us

Please address comments and questions concerning this book to the publisher:

  O'Reilly Media, Inc.
  1005 Gravenstein Highway North
  Sebastopol, CA 95472
  800-998-9938 (in the United States or Canada)
  707-829-0515 (international or local)
  707 829-0104 (fax)

We have a web page for this book, where we list errata, examples, and any additional information. You can access this page at:

http://www.oreilly.com/catalog/9780596519780

To comment or ask technical questions about this book, send email to:

bookquestions@oreilly.com

For more information about our books, conferences, Resource Centers, and the O'Reilly Network, see our web site at:

http://www.oreilly.com

Safari® Enabled

 When you see a Safari® Enabled icon on the cover of your favorite technology book, that means the book is available online through the O'Reilly Network Safari Bookshelf.

Safari offers a solution that's better than e-books. It's a virtual library that lets you easily search thousands of top tech books, cut and paste code samples, download chapters, and find quick answers when you need the most accurate, current information. Try it for free at *http://safari.oreilly.com.*

Acknowledgments

This is the only part of the book my non-techy friends will read, so I'd better make it good. My entire life-support system has helped me greatly in this long, drawn-out book process. First, my family, especially my mom Hazel and dad Geary, but also my entire extended family, including my stepmother Sherrie and my stepdad Lloyd. The No Fluff, Just Stuff speakers, attendees, and the organizer Jay Zimmerman have helped me vet this material over many months, and the speakers in particular make the ridiculous amount of travel worthwhile. A special thanks goes to my ThoughtWorks colleagues: a group of people with whom I feel extraordinarily privileged to work. I've never before seen a company as committed to revolutionizing the way people write software, with such highly intelligent, passionate, dedicated, selfless people. I attribute at least some of this to the extraordinary Roy Singham, the founder of ThoughtWorks, and upon whom I have a bit of a man-crush, I think. Thanks to all my neighbors (both the non-garage and honorary garage ones), who don't know or care about any of this technology stuff, especially Kitty Lee, Diane and Jamie Coll, Betty Smith, and all the other current and former Executive Park neighbors (and yes that includes you Margie). Special thanks to my friends that now extend around the globe: Masoud Kamali, Frank Stepan, Sebastian Meyen, and the rest of the S&S crew. And, of course, the guys I see only in other countries, like Michael Li, and, even though they live only five miles away, Terry Dietzler and his wife Stacy, whose schedules far too rarely line up with mine. Thanks (even though they can't read this) to Isabella, Winston, and Parker, who don't care about technology but really care about attention (on their terms, of course). A thanks to my friend Chuck, whose increasingly rare visits still manage to lighten my day. And, saving the most important for last, my wonderful wife Candy. All my speaker friends claim that she's a saint for allowing me to gallivant around the world, speaking about and writing software. She has graciously indulged my all-encompassing career because she knows I love it, but not as much as her. She's patiently waiting around until I retire or tire of all this, and I can spend all my time with her.

CHAPTER ONE

Introduction

PRODUCTIVITY IS DEFINED AS THE AMOUNT OF USEFUL WORK PERFORMED OVER TIME. Someone who is more productive performs more effective work in a given time interval than someone less productive. This book is all about how to become more productive as you go about the tasks required to develop software. It is language and operating system agnostic: I provide tips in a variety of languages, and across three major operating systems: Windows (in various flavors), Mac OS X, and *-nix (Unix and Linux alternatives).

This book is about individual programmer productivity, not group productivity. To that end, I don't talk about methodology (well, maybe a little here and there, but always on the periphery). I also don't discuss productivity gains that affect the whole team. My mission is to allow individual programmers the tools and philosophies to get more useful work done per unit of time.

Why a Book on Programmer Productivity?

I work for ThoughtWorks, an international consulting company of about 1,000 employees spread across 6 countries. Because we are traveling consultants (especially in the U.S.), we are a demographically very young company. It came to pass at one of our company outings (where beverages were served) that I starting chatting with one of the People people. She asked me how old I was and I told her. Then, she gave me an off-handed compliment(?): "Wow, you're old enough to add diversity to the company!" That sparked some thoughts. I've been developing software for many years (cue the maudlin "Back in my day, we had kerosene-powered computers..."). During that time, I've observed an interesting phenomenon: developers are getting less efficient, not more. Back in ancient times (a couple of decades in computer time), *running* a computer was a difficult job, much less programming the thing. You had to be a really clever developer to get anything useful from the beastly machine. This crucible forged Really Smart Guys who developed all sorts of efficient ways to interact with the intractable computers of their age.

Slowly, due to the hard work of programmers, computers became easier to use. This innovation was really to stop users from complaining so much. The Really Smart Guys congratulated themselves (as all programmers do when they can get a user to pipe down). Then a funny thing happened: a whole generation of developers came along who no longer needed clever tricks and devious intelligence to get computers to do what they wanted. The developers, like the end users, basked in the easier-to-use computers. So, what's wrong with that? After all, productivity is a good thing, right?

It depends. What is productive for a user (nice graphical user interface, mice, pull-down menus, etc.) can actually be a hindrance to someone trying to get the best performance from a computer. "Easy to use" and "efficient" overlap infrequently. Developers who grew up using graphical user interfaces (OK, I'll just go ahead and say it: Windows) don't know many of the cool, efficient tricks of the trade of the Really Smart Guys of yesteryear. Developers today are not *running* their computers, they are *walking* them. I'm going to try to fix that.

Address Completion in Browsers

Here's a quick example: how many web sites do you visit in a day? Most of them start with "www." and end with ".com". A little-known shortcut exists for all modern browsers: *address completion*. Address completion uses a hotkey combination to automatically add "www." to the beginning and ".com" to the end of the string you type in the browser's address bar. Different browsers support slightly different syntax. (Note that this is different from letting the browser automatically supply the prefix and suffix. All the modern browsers do that too.) The difference is one of efficiency. To autocomplete the prefix and suffix, the browser goes out to the network and looks for a site with the "bare" name. If it doesn't find one, it tries it with the prefix and suffix, entailing another trip out to the network. With a fast connection, you may not even notice the lag, but you're slowing down the whole Internet with all those false hits!

Internet Explorer

Internet Explorer (IE) makes it easier to type in addresses that contain standard prefixes and suffixes. Use the keys Ctrl-Enter to add "www." to the front of an address and ".com" to the end.

Firefox

The same Internet Explorer shortcut works for the Windows version of Firefox as well. For Macintosh, Apple-Enter does the same thing. Firefox goes one better: for all the platforms it supports, Alt-Enter places a ".org" at the end.

Firefox has other handy shortcut keys that no one seems to leverage. To go directly to a tab, you can use Ctrl + <TAB-NUMBER> in Windows or Apple + <TAB-NUMBER> in OS X.

OK, this shortcut is worth a measly eight keystrokes per web page. But think of the number of web pages you visit every day, and those eight characters per page start to add up. This is an example of the principle of *acceleration*, defined in Chapter 2.

But saving eight keystrokes per web page isn't the point of this example. I conducted an informal poll of all the developers I know and learned that less than 20 percent of them knew this shortcut. These folks are hardcore computer experts, yet they weren't taking advantage of even the simplest productivity gains. My mission is to rectify that.

What This Book Is About

The Productive Programmer is divided into two parts. The first discusses the *mechanics* of productivity, and the tools and their uses that make you more productive as you go through the physical activities of developing software. The second part discusses the *practice* of productivity, and how you can leverage your knowledge and the knowledge of others to produce better software more quickly. In both sections, you will likely run into some things you already know, as well as things you have never thought of before.

Part I: Mechanics (The Productivity Principles)

You can treat this book as a recipe book for command-line and other productivity tips and still reap benefits. But if you understand *why* something increases productivity, you can recognize it all around you. Creating patterns to describe something creates *nomenclature*: once you have a name for something, it's easier to recognize when you see it again. One of the goals of this book is to define a set of productivity principles to help you define your own productivity techniques. Like all patterns, it becomes easier to identify them once they have names. Knowing why something speeds you up allows you to more quickly identify other things that will help you work faster.

This is not just a book on how to use computers more effectively (although that is a side effect). It is focused on *programmer* productivity. To this end, I don't cover many things that are obvious to casual or even power users (although, as the exception that proves the rule, the earlier section "Address Completion in Browsers" does show an obvious tip). Programmers represent a unique subsection of computer users. We should be able to bend computers to our will more effectively than anyone else because we understand the most about how they really work. Mostly, this book is about things you can do with and to a computer to make your job easier, faster, and more efficient. However, I also discuss some low-hanging fruit that can make you more productive.

Part I covers every productivity tip I could invent, harvest, bully out of my friends, or read about. Originally, I aimed to create the world's most awesome collection of productivity recipes. I don't know if that happened, but you will still find a pretty impressive collection of recipes here.

As I started collating all these cool productivity tips, I noticed patterns emerging. Looking over these techniques, I started formulating categories of productivity for programmers. Eventually, I created the *Principles of Programmer Productivity* because, frankly, I couldn't think of a more pretentious name. These principles are *acceleration*, *focus*, *automation*, and *canonicality*. They describe the practices that allow programmers to become more productive.

Chapter 2, *Acceleration*, describes becoming more productive by speeding something up. Obviously, if one person is faster at a particular task, that person is more productive at that task than someone who goes more slowly doing the same thing. Great examples of the acceleration principle are the numerous keyboard shortcuts that appear throughout the book. Acceleration encompasses things like launching applications, managing clipboards, and searching and navigation.

Chapter 3, *Focus*, describes how to achieve the state of super-productivity, using both tools and environmental factors. It discusses ways to reduce the clutter of your environment (both physical and virtual), how to search efficiently, and how to avoid distractions.

Getting the computer to perform extra work for you obviously makes you more productive. Chapter 4, *Automation*, describes coercing your computer to do more work for you. Many of the tasks you perform every day can (and should) be automated. This chapter has examples and strategies to put your computer to work.

Canonicality is really just a fancy term for the application of the DRY (Don't Repeat Yourself) principle, first espoused in *The Pragmatic Programmer* (Addison-Wesley) by Andy Hunt and Dave Thomas. The DRY principle advises programmers to find places where information is duplicated and create a single source for this information. *The Pragmatic Programmer* eloquently describes this principle, and in Chapter 5, *Canonicality*, I show concrete examples of applying it.

Part II: Practice (Philosophy)

I've worked as a consultant for most of my many seasoned years as a developer. Consultants have advantages over developers who work on the same code base year after year. We get to see lots of different projects and lots of different approaches. Of course, we see our share of train wrecks as well (rarely do consultants get called in to "fix" healthy projects). We get to see the broad spectrum of software development: building things from the start, advising in the middle, and rescuing what's badly broken. Over time, even the least observant person can get a feel for what works and what doesn't.

Part II is the distillation of the things I've seen that either make developers more productive or detract from their productivity. I've bundled them together in a more or less random order (although you may be surprised by how often the same ideas come up in different guises). This isn't meant to be the ultimate compendium of things that make developers productive; rather, it is the list of things I've observed, which is just a small subset of the possibilities.

Where to Go Now?

The two parts of this book stand alone, so you can read them in any order; however, Part II is a tad more narrative, and unexpected connections may pop up. Still, most of the material in it is nonsequential: you can read it in any order you like.

One note of warning. If you aren't comfortable with basic command-line stuff (pipes, redirection, etc.), you should make a quick visit to Appendix A. It covers getting an environment set up that is suitable for using many of the tricks and techniques discussed in Part I. It's pretty painless, I promise.

PART I

Mechanics

Part I, *Mechanics*, deals with (yup, you guessed it) the mechanics of productivity. Many of these tools aren't necessarily developer tools, but rather tools that could be of help to any sophisticated power user. Of course, developers should be the ultimate power users, taking full advantage of virtually all the tool categories listed in this part of the book.

CHAPTER TWO

Acceleration

USING A COMPUTER REQUIRES A FAIR AMOUNT OF RITUAL AND CEREMONY. You have to boot it up, you have to know how to launch applications, and you must understand the interaction model, which can differ between applications. The less you interact with your computer, the faster you can go. In other words, eliminating ceremony allows you more time to get to the essence of the problem. Time you spend digging through a long filesystem hierarchy to find something is time you could be using to be more productive. Computers are tools, and the more time you spend on the care and feeding of the tool, the less work you get done. The science fiction author Douglas Adams had a great quote: "We are stuck with technology when what we really want is just stuff that works."

> **NOTE**
> Concentrate on essence, not ceremony.

This chapter is all about figuring out ways to accelerate your interaction with your computer, whether it's launching applications more quickly, finding files faster, or using the mouse less.

Launching Pad

Take a look at your computer's list of applications. If you are using Windows, click on Start and choose Programs. How many columns do you have? Two? Three? Four!? As hard drives have gotten bigger and the kinds of applications (and therefore the tools we must use) have gotten more complex, the number of applications we use has exploded. Of course, with commonplace 100 GB drives, we can pack lots of stuff into our systems. But volume exacts a price.

> **NOTE**
> The usefulness of an application list is inversely proportional to its length.

The longer the list, the less useful it becomes. With three columns in Windows or a dock that squeezes items to microscopic size in Mac OS X, it's getting harder and harder to find what we need. This hits developers particularly hard because we have lots of *occasional applications*: special-purpose tools that we may run only one day a month, but that we desperately need when that day arrives.

Launchers

Launchers are applications that allow you to type the first part of the name of an application (or document) to launch it. Most of the time, this is a more efficient way to launch applications.

> **NOTE**
> Eye candy looks good but isn't nutritious.

If you know the name of the thing you are after (like the name of the application), why not just tell your computer what you want, rather than sort through a massive list or search for it in a sea of icons? Launchers cut through the graphical eye candy and drill precisely and quickly to the thing you need.

All the major operating systems have open source and free launchers that allow you to type the name (or a portion of the name) of the application you want to launch. A few that are worth trying are Launchy,[*] Colibri,[†] and Enso.[‡] Both Launchy and Colibri are open source and therefore free, and they both allow you to open a small window and start typing the name of your application, which will pop up on a list. Launchy is currently the most popular of the open source launchers. Colibri is attempting to reproduce a Mac OS X utility called Quicksilver (discussed in the upcoming section "Mac OS X").

Enso is a launcher with some interesting added features. It is also free (but not open source), created by Humanized, the company founded by Jef Raskin, one of the early user interface designers for the Mac. Enso encapsulates many of his (sometimes slightly radical) user interface views, but it is quite effective. For example, one of the ideas that Raskin promotes is the idea of Quasimode keys, which act like the Shift key (in other words, changing the mode of the keyboard when held down). Enso takes over the pretty worthless Caps Lock key and uses it to launch applications and perform other tasks. You hold the Caps Lock key down and start typing a command, like *OPEN FIREFOX*, and it will open Firefox. Of course, that is cumbersome to type, so another Enso command is *LEARN AS FF FIREFOX*, which teaches Enso that the *FF* command launches Firefox. Enso does more than just launching. If you have a math expression like 4+3 in a document, you can highlight it and invoke the *CALCULATE* command, and Enso will replace your highlighted text with the value of the calculation. Enso is worth trying to see if Raskin's views on launching mesh with yours.

If you are using Windows Vista, it includes the launching part of these launcher applications. When you invoke Start, the bottom of the ensuing menu has a search field, allowing you to type the name of the application you want, using incremental searching. But it has one disadvantage (perhaps a bug) that the launchers mentioned above don't have: if you type something that doesn't exist, Windows Vista takes a very long time to come back and tell you that it can't find it. Your machine is about as useful as a brick while this is happening. Hopefully, this is just a quirk in the current version and will be fixed soon.

[*] Download at *http://www.launchy.net.*

[†] Download at *http://colibri.leetspeak.org.*

[‡] Download at *http://www.humanized.com.*

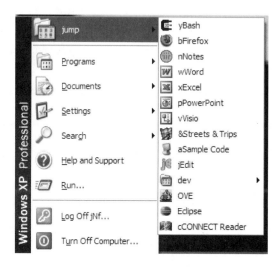

FIGURE 2-1. Custom launcher window

Creating a Windows Launching Pad

You can easily take advantage of the folder infrastructure in Windows to create your own launching pad. Create a folder under the Start button that contains shortcuts to the applications you use on a daily basis. You might call this folder "jump" and use "j" as its shortcut key, so you can access it by typing Windows-J. An example of just such a "jump" window appears in Figure 2-1. Notice that each of the menu items includes a single-letter prefix that is unique within the folder, which facilitates launching applications fast. Every application in the launch folder is just two keystrokes away: Windows-J[<unique letter>] launches the application.

This is just a directory, so you can nest other directories inside it to create your own mini-hierarchy of applications. For most of my workhorse machines, 26 entries isn't enough, so I tend to create a *dev* launch folder that contains all the development tools. I'm willfully trading one hierarchy for another, but with a big difference: I have complete control over this organization, unlike the Programs group in Windows. I regularly reorganize this folder as some applications fall out of favor and new ones take their place.

Creating the launching folder is very simple, but it depends on the flavor of Start button you have. Windows XP and Vista support two kinds of "Start" configurations: "classic" (the style from Windows 95 through 2000) and "modern" (Windows XP and Vista). For "classic" Windows, creating the launch folder is extremely simple. Right-click on the Start button, choose either Open (if you just want to add a launch menu for the currently logged-in user) or Open All Users (to change it for everyone). This opens the underlying folder that controls the contents of the "Start" menu, where you can add shortcuts to your heart's content. Alternatively, you can go to where the Start menu lives, under the current user's Documents and Settings directory structure. An easy way to fill up your launch menu with just the stuff you need all the time is to select them from the massive Programs menu and right-drag them into your launch folder, creating a copy of the shortcut.

If you have the "modern" Windows Start menu, creating a launch menu is tougher, but still possible. You can create the launch folder in the same directory as mentioned earlier, but for some odd reason, it no longer appears right when you hit the Windows key; it now appears only after you expand the Programs group. This is a major annoyance because now our accelerated way to launch stuff takes an extra keystroke; however, there is a way around this problem. If you create your *jump* folder on the desktop and drag-drop it onto the Start menu, it will create a folder that shows up right away. The only remaining headache with the "modern" version of the Start menu concerns the hotkey. In the "modern" menu, different applications move in and out, depending on usage (Windows randomizes your carefully memorized paths to get to things quickly). So, if you use the "modern" Start menu, you should choose a first character for your launch menu that won't conflict, like the ~ or (keys.

Because it is such as hassle, I tend to just use the "classic" version of the Start button. You can change from "modern" to "classic" in either Windows XP or Vista via the properties of the taskbar, as shown in Figure 2-2.

RE-WIRING SPECIAL FOLDERS IN WINDOWS

Microsoft issues (but doesn't support) a collection of utilities known as PowerToys,[§] including Tweak UI, which lets you make changes to your Windows registry through a graphical interface. My Documents normally resides at the knuckle-bending location of *c:\Documents and Settings\<your login name>\My Documents* (mercifully changed to just *Documents*, directly off the root in Windows Vista). Tweak UI allows you to change the default location of My Documents so that you can move it to a more sane location like *c:\Documents* (where Windows Vista puts your documents by default).

Be careful, though: if you are going to move My Documents, you should do it early in the life of your install of the operating system. Lots of Windows applications rely on artifacts in that directory, and you will subsequently break lots of applications if you do this on a well-established Windows machine.

If you don't want to go quite this far, you can select a folder (like My Documents), right-click to get the properties dialog, and tell Windows to relocate it. It will copy all your My Documents files to the new location. You can also use the ancient *subst* command (which allows you to substitute one folder for another), but it is known to break lots of applications, so use it with caution. Junction, a utility that lets you truly substitute one directory for another, works better if you are using the NTFS filesystem. See "Indirection" in Chapter 5 for more details.

---

§ Download at *http://www.microsoft.com/windowsxp/downloads/powertoys/xppowertoys.mspx.*

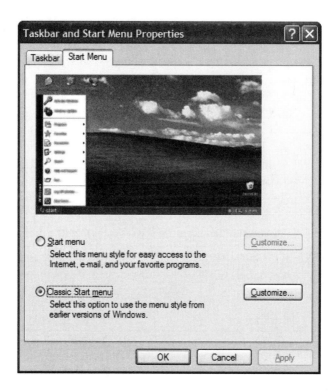

FIGURE 2-2. Changing back to the classic menu

Windows does have a quick and easy mechanism that serves as a launcher for a few applications: the Quick Launch bar. This is the shortcut area that appears on your task bar, typically beside the Start button. If you don't see it, you'll have to turn it on by right-clicking on the taskbar and choosing the Quick Launch bar. You can drag-and-drop shortcuts here and use it as a launcher. And, because this is a directory (like everything else), you can place things directly in the Quick Launch folder. Just like all other shortcuts, you may assign operating system–wide key accelerators to these items, but existing application accelerators will interfere with them.

> NOTE
> Typing is faster than navigation.

Windows Vista has a slightly new twist to the Quick Launch bar. You can run the applications associated with the shortcut via the Windows-<NUM> keysym. In other words, Windows-1 selects and presses the first Quick Launch item, Windows-2 launches the second, and so on. This mechanism works great…as long as you have only 10 applications that you use regularly! While this won't accommodate as many applications as a real launcher, it might be a handy place to put a few critically important applications.

WHY NOT JUST ASSIGN HOTKEYS TO YOUR FAVORITE APPLICATIONS?

All the major operating systems allow you to create keyboard accelerators (that is, hotkeys) to launch applications. So, why not just define a list of accelerators and be done with all this launching business? Mapping hotkeys to application launching works great if you always have the desktop as the current focus. But developers virtually never have only the desktop (or filesystem explorer) open. Typically, a developer has 20 special-purpose tools open, each with its own magic keyboard combination. Trying to use the operating system's hotkeys to launch applications contributes to this Tower of Babel effect. It is virtually impossible to find hotkeys that don't interfere with at least some of your currently open applications. While using operating system–level hotkeys sounds like an attractive idea, it falls down in practical use.

Mac OS X

Mac OS X's *dock* combines the utility of the quick start menu and the task buttons in Windows. It encourages you to place oft-needed applications on the dock, and drag the others off into space (with a satisfying "poof" when they disappear). Just like with the quick start bar, the constraints of real estate hurt you: placing a useful number of applications on the dock expands it to the point where it becomes cumbersome. This has created a cottage industry of alternative launchers for Mac OS X. Even though some well-known launchers have been around for years, most power users today have migrated to Quicksilver.

Quicksilver[||] is the closest anyone has come to creating a graphical command line. Just like a bash prompt, Quicksilver allows you to launch applications, perform file maintenance, and a host of other behaviors. Quicksilver itself appears as a floating window, invoked via a customizable hotkey (everything about Quicksilver is customizable, including the look and feel of the floating window). Once it appears, you can perform actions in the "target" pane.

GETTING QUICKSILVER

Quicksilver is currently free, downloadable from *http://quicksilver.blacktree.com/*. Quicksilver's creator is actively encouraging developers to build more plug-ins for it. There are plug-ins for Subversion, PathFinder, Automator, and tons of other applications, both core operating system and third-party.

Quicksilver is absolutely addictive. More than any other piece of software, it has fundamentally changed the way I interact with my computer. Quicksilver represents that rarest of commodities in

[||] Download at *http://quicksilver.blacktree.com/*.

software: simple elegance. The first time you see it, you think "No big deal, just a new way to launch applications." The more you use it, however, the more subtlety you see, and the more its power gradually reveals itself.

Quicksilver makes it easy to launch applications via a hotkey and a couple of keystrokes. You get three panes in Quicksilver: the top one for files or applications ("nouns"), the middle for actions ("verbs"), and the third (if necessary) for the target of the action ("direct object"). When you search for items in Quicksilver, it treats everything you type as it if had a universal wildcard character. For example, if you type "shcmem" in Quicksilver, it will locate a file named *ShoppingCartMemento.java*.

Quicksilver doesn't just launch applications. It allows you to apply any (context-sensitive) command to any file. In Figure 2-3, I've selected a file named *acceleration_quicksilver_regex.tiff* and I've specified the Move To… action. The third pane allows me to choose the destination for the move, in the same manner that I chose the filename in the target pane (that is, using the special wildcard behavior described earlier).

FIGURE 2-3. Quicksilver's third pane indicates a move target

Why is this such a big deal for developers? Quicksilver works via plug-ins, and a fair number of developer-centric plug-ins exist. For example, Quicksilver features excellent Subversion integration. You can update repositories, commit changes, get status, and a whole bunch of other functions. While not as powerful as command-line Subversion (nothing really compares to that), it gives you a quick graphical way to do common chores with just a few keystrokes.

One other thing about Quicksilver is worth mentioning: *triggers*. A trigger is a noun-verb-direct object combination, just as you would do it via the normal user interface, stored permanently under a hotkey. For example, I have several projects that I use the same sequence of keys for all the time:

1. Invoke Quicksilver
2. Choose the directory of the project (the noun)
3. Choose the "Open with…" action (the verb)
4. Choose TextMate as the application (the direct object)

I do this so often I've assigned a trigger to it. Now, with a single keystroke (Alt-1 in my case), I can invoke this sequence of commands. Triggers are designed to allow you to save common Quicksilver operations under a single hotkey. I also use triggers for things like starting and stopping servlet engines (like Tomcat and Jetty). Very useful indeed.

I've only scratched the surface of Quicksilver's capabilities. You can launch applications, apply commands to one or multiple files, switch songs in iTunes, and tons of other stuff. It changes the way you use the operating system. With Quicksilver, you can use the dock just as a task manager, showing the currently running applications, and use Quicksilver as the launcher. Quicksilver customization happens through a published plug-in API (see the previous sidebar "Getting Quicksilver" for information about how to download Quicksilver and its plug-ins).

Quicksilver is a great example of an application that looks too simple to be useful when you first install it. Numerous friends have said to me "I installed Quicksilver, now what do I do?" To that end, some friends and I created a blog around general productivity topics on the Mac, called PragMactic-OSXer (*http://pragmactic-osxer.blogspot.com*).

WHY NOT JUST USE SPOTLIGHT?

The functionality of Quicksilver overlaps that of Spotlight, the built-in search facility on Mac OS X. But Quicksilver is much more than just quick search. It allows you to essentially replace the Mac OS X Finder, because all typical file manipulation is done more quickly in Quicksilver (typing is faster than navigating). Quicksilver allows you to specify what items you want to catalog (unlike Spotlight indexing your entire hard drive), making Quicksilver faster at finding files in its index. And Quicksilver uses the cool "regex between every character" way of specifying search items, which Spotlight doesn't. I virtually never use Finder anymore. All file operations (and pretty much all interaction with my computer) happen through Quicksilver. I've become so dependent on it that if it ever crashes (which happens rarely but does happen; it's still in beta, after all), it's as if my machine has been suddenly crippled. More than any other utility I've ever used, it has changed the way I work.

Leopard's version of Spotlight is much faster than previous versions, but of course these two tools aren't mutually exclusive. In Leopard's version of Spotlight, you can now do searches across multiple machines (which Quicksilver won't do). For this to work, you must be logged into the other machine (for obvious security reasons). Now, when you perform a Spotlight search, you can choose on the toolbar which machine you want to search. In the example shown in Figure 2-4, from my laptop I've logged onto the desktop machine (called *Neal-office*) and selected the home directory (named *nealford*). When I do the Spotlight search, I can choose the target in the toolbar at the top. The file *music.rb* exists only on the desktop machine.

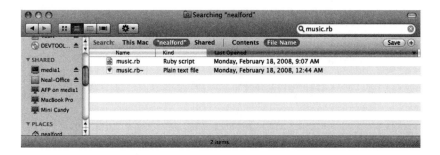

FIGURE 2-4. *Spotlight on Leopard allows cross-machine searching*

Unfortunately, the Windows and Linux worlds don't have anything quite as spectacular as Quicksilver. The aforementioned Colibri implements a small percentage of Quicksilver's functionality (mostly around its launching ability, but not the graphical command-line part). Hopefully, someone will eventually either port Quicksilver to other platforms or create a convincing clone of it. It is far and away the most sophisticated launcher of any operating system.

Launching in Linux

Most desktop Linuxes run either GNOME or KDE. Both have similar taskbar style user interfaces borrowed from Windows. However, it is considerably more difficult to customize their start options because their menu structures don't exist as simple directory entries. Modern versions of GNOME include a pretty functional launcher, tied by default to the Alt-F2 keysym. It shows a list of the runnable applications and allows you to refine your selection via typing. In Figure 2-5, the list is narrowed by the two letters "fi."

Accelerators

NOTE
Prefer typing over mousing.

Developers are essentially specialized data entry clerks. Instead of coming from some external source, the data we enter into the computer comes from our heads. But the lessons of data entry operators still resonate. Data entry workers who are paid for the amount of information

FIGURE 2-5. GNOME's "Run Application" launcher

they can input know that using the mouse slows them down by orders of magnitude. Developers can learn an important lesson here.

The classic "No Mouse Required" application is the VI editor. Watching an experienced VI user inspires awe. The cursor seems to follow their eyes. Unfortunately, it takes about two years of daily VI usage to get to that point because the learning curve is so daunting. If you've used it every day for 1 year and 364 days, you'll still struggle. The other classic Unix editor is Emacs, which is also very keyboard-centric. Emacs, though, is the proto-IDE: through its plug-in architecture, it does a lot more than just edit files. VI users scornfully refer to Emacs as "a great operating system with limited text-editing capabilities."

Both VI and Emacs support a very important accelerator: never taking your hands off the character keys. Even reaching down to the arrow keys on a keyboard slows you down because you must return to the home row keys to type characters again. Really useful editors keep your hands in optimum position to input and navigate at the same time.

Short of learning VI, you can figure out how to use *accelerators* to speed up your interaction with both the operating system and its applications. This section describes some ways to accelerate your use of both underlying operating systems and tools like IDEs. I start at the operating system–level and work my way up the food chain toward IDEs.

Operating System Accelerators

Graphical operating systems favor convenience (and eye candy) over raw efficiency. The command line is still the most efficient way to interact with a computer because very little stands between the user and the desired result. Still, most modern operating systems support a plethora of keyboard shortcuts and other navigation aids to help speed up your work.

Windows address bar

One of the great navigation aids on command lines is autocompletion, where you hit the Tab key and the shell automatically completes the matching element in the current directory. If more than one match occurs, it generates the common parts and allows you to add more characters to complete a full name of something (a directory, a filename, etc.). All the major operating systems have completion on command lines now, usually using the Tab character.

WHAT IF I'M STILL RUNNING WINDOWS 2000?

Even though Windows 2000 doesn't perform tab filename completion at the command line by default, it is a simple registry tweak away. To enable filename completion in Windows 2000:

1. Run regedit.

2. Navigate to *HKEY_CURRENT_USER\Software\Microsoft\Command Processor*.

3. Make a DWORD value EnableExtensions, equal to 1.

4. Make a DWORD value CompletionChar, equal to 9.

Many developers don't realize that Windows Explorer's address bar also offers Tab filename completion, exactly like a command prompt. The keyboard shortcut to get to the address bar is Alt-D; from there, you can start typing part of a directory, hit Tab, and Explorer will complete the name for you.

Mac OS X Finder

Mac OS X includes a huge number of keyboard shortcuts, and each application has a set of its own. Ironically enough, considering Apple's general concern for usability, OS X applications aren't as consistent as those in most Windows applications. Microsoft has done a great job of creating and enforcing some common standards, and key mapping has probably been its biggest success. Nevertheless, Mac OS X has some nice built-in keyboard shortcuts and others that aren't immediately apparent. Like much around the Mac, it takes someone showing you many of these before you discover them.

A perfect example of this is keyboard navigation in both Finder and in open/save dialogs. In Windows Explorer, the address bar is obvious. In Finder, though, you can use tab completion to navigate to any folder (just like using the address bar in Explorer) by typing Apple-Shift-G, which displays a dialog into which you can type the location.

You shouldn't use either Finder or the terminal exclusively (see "Command Prompts at Your Fingertips," later in this chapter). They interact quite nicely with one another. You can drag folders from Finder into Terminal for a quick way to issue a *cd* command. You can also use the *open* command to open files from Terminal rather than double-clicking them in Finder. It's all about context and learning the capabilities of the tools at hand so that you can apply those capabilities appropriately.

> NOTE
> Take the time to learn all the hidden keyboard shortcuts of your universe.

Shortcuts that Windows users miss a lot on Mac OS X are the Alt key accelerators for applications. Mac OS has them, but they're based on incremental search rather than explicit key relationships. The Ctrl-F2 key moves focus up to the menu bar, and you can type the first part of the menu item you want. When it's highlighted, hit Enter and start incrementally typing the enclosed menu item. It sounds complicated, but it works beautifully, and it works across all applications. You can also use Ctrl-F8 to move the focus to the far right of the menu bar, where all the services icons live.

My biggest problem with this was the cumbersome gymnastics needed to invoke Ctrl-F2, so I used the standard Mac OS X keyboard shortcut dialog to remap it to Ctrl-Alt-Apple-Spacebar (which sounds even worse, but they all line up, so it's an easy combination to hit). Plus, my Quicksilver invoker is mapped to Apple-Enter, so all my "meta" navigation is mapped to more or less the same general area.

If you are using the latest version of Mac OS X, choosing menu items is even easier. One of Leopard's help features finds menu items for you when you type the name (or just part of the name). This is a great way to access menu items that live in deeply nested menus, ones whose names you remember but whose locations evade you, and things that you think the application should do but you don't know where the functionality lives. If you hit the Apple-? key, the help search option will appear. Type any part of the menu item name you want, and Leopard will highlight it for you and invoke it if you hit Enter. As is the case with much keyboard magic, it is harder to explain than to do (Figure 2-6).

Clipboard(s)

It is sometimes amazing how far backward we can fall. Both of the legendary editors of yesteryear (VI and Emacs) have multiple clipboards (also called registers). Yet, the two major operating systems limit us to a measly single clipboard. You'd think that clipboards were a scarce natural resource that must be doled out carefully lest we run out someday. This is a perfect example of how much useful information we lose from generation to generation of

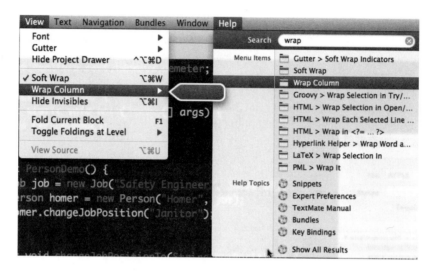

FIGURE 2-6. *Leopard finds menu items for you*

developers because of insufficient lore between groups. We keep reinventing the same things over and over because we don't realize that someone already solved the problem a decade ago.

NOTE
Context switching eats time.

Having multiple clipboards may not seem like a big productivity gain. But once you get accustomed to having them, it changes the way you work. For example, if a task requires copying and pasting several disjoint items from one file to another, most developers will copy, bounce to the other file, paste, bounce back to the first one, and repeat ad nauseum. Clearly, this isn't a productive way to work. You end up spending too much time context switching between the open applications. If you have a clipboard *stack*, however, you can harvest all the values from the first file—stacking them up on your clipboards—then bounce once to the destination file and paste them all in the appropriate places, one at a time.

NOTE
Clipboarding in batches is faster than clipboarding serially.

It's interesting how such a simple mechanism takes time to internalize. Even when you install a multi-clipboard utility, it takes a while before you realize all the situations where it applies. Too often, you install it and promptly forget it's there. Like with many of the productivity hints in this book, you have to keep an active mindset to take advantage of these techniques. Recognizing the appropriate situation where one of them applies is half the battle. I constantly use clipboard history; I can't imagine life without it now.

Fortunately, there are a variety of clipboard enhancers available for both Windows and Mac OS X, both open source and commercial. A nice, bare-bones open source alternative in Windows is CLCL,[#] which gives you a configurable clipboard stack and allows you to assign your own keyboard shortcuts. For Mac OS X, JumpCut[*] is a simple, open source clipboard stack. For a more elaborate (commercial) offering, jClip[†] is very nice, allowing you not only a clipboard stack but also a configurable number of clipboards, distinct from one another. Having unique clipboards is nice if you have a large group of items you are copying and you don't want to pollute your main clipboard stack.

Be careful when you get accustomed to using a clipboard stack, though. You might exuberantly start talking about it to a be-sandaled Unix guy, causing an hour-long lecture about how he's had multiple clipboards since you were in grammar school and all the other ways that 20-year-old text editors rule.

Remember History

NOTE
Those who remember their history aren't doomed to type it again.

All shells have a history mechanism, which allows you to recall previous commands and repeat them, with changes if necessary. This is one of the huge advantages that shells have over graphical environments: you can't repeat actions with subtle changes easily in graphical environments. Thus, learning to perform operations at the command prompt means that you have a more effective communication layer between yourself and the machine.

History is generally wired to the up and down arrow keys, which is a brute-force way to get to previous commands. But, as I've stated before, searching is more effective than navigation. You can search your history to find the command in question faster than you can scan each entry as you walk back through them one at a time.

In Windows, type the first part of the previous command and then hit F8. The shell will perform a backward search through previous commands that match the first part nof what you've just typed. You can keep hitting the F8 key to continue walking up the list of matching commands. If you want to see the command history, type F7, which shows your recent history in a list where you can utilize the up and down arrow keys to select the command.

On Unix-based systems (including Cygwin), you can choose which type of command-line key syntax you want, either Emacs (usually the default) or VI. As I mentioned previously, VI is a

---

[#] Download at *http://www.nakka.com/soft/clcl/index_eng.html.*

[*] Download at *http://jumpcut.sourceforge.net/.*

[†] Download at *http://inventive.us/iClip/.*

super powerful navigation keyset, but it is very daunting to learn from scratch. You can set VI mode in your *-nix environment by adding the following to your ~/.profile file:

```
set -o vi
```

When you have VI mode set, you can hit Escape (which puts you in command mode), then / to put yourself in search mode. Type the search text, then hit Enter. The first match will be the most recent command that matches the search string. If that's not the one you want, hit / followed by Enter to search for the next occurrence. Also in bash, if you have recently executed a command, you can hit the hotkey ! along with the first letter of the recent command to re-run it. The ! gives you access to the history directly. If you want to see your command-line history, execute the *history* command, which provides a numbered list of the commands you've executed, in reverse order (in other words, the most recent command is at the bottom of the list). You can execute commands from the history using an exclamation point (!) + the history number of the command you want. This is great if you have some complex command you want to re-execute.

There and Back

As developers, we constantly jump around the filesystem. We always need to grab a JAR file, go find some documentation, copy an assembly, or install a foo over at the bar. Consequently, we must hone our navigation and targeting skills. As I've preached for a while in this chapter, graphical explorers and finders are poorly suited to that kind of jumping around (because it's never just a jump…it's a round trip somewhere to handle some little chore, because we'll have to go back to where we started).

HIDDEN ALT-TAB ENTRIES

The Alt-Tab viewer in Windows holds only 21 items. Once you've exceeded that number, they just stop showing up (even though the applications are still running). You can either control your Explorer spawning or follow one of these two solutions, both involving Windows PowerToys. The first is Tweak UI, which allows you to configure the number of items that appear in the Alt-Tab dialog. The other solution involves installing multiple desktops through the Virtual Desktop PowerToy, which I discuss in "Segregate Your Workspace with Virtual Desktops," in Chapter 3.

Mac OS X allows you to kill instances of applications while you are Apple-Tab'ing around… just hit the Q key with the doomed application focused and it will close. Similarly, if you use the application manager Witch, you can kill individual windows using the W key while the window is focused, which is great for killing Finder windows left and right. Of course, if you use Quicksilver, you don't need Finder windows as much.

A couple of old-school command-line tools offer a good alternative to spawning new Explorers every time you need to jump to another location. They allow you to navigate temporarily to another location, do whatever needs to be done, and then return to where you started. *pushd* performs two actions: it puts you in the directory you've passed as an argument and pushes the current directory into an internal stack. *pushd* is therefore an alternative to the more pedestrian *cd* command. Once you've finished your work, issue a *popd* command to return to the original location.

pushd and *popd* work on a directory stack. This is a stack in the computer science sense, meaning that it acts as a FILO (First In, Last Out) list (the classic, well-worn analogy is a stack of dishes in a cafeteria). Because it is a stack, you can "push" as many times as you want, and they will "pop" back off in the reverse order.

All Unixes have the *pushd* and *popd* commands (including Mac OS X). However, they aren't some esoteric Cygwin-only adjunct to Windows.

```
[jNf| ~/work ]=> pushd ~/Documents/
~/Documents ~/work
[jNf| ~/Documents ]=> pushd /opt/local/lib/ruby/1.8
/opt/local/lib/ruby/1.8 ~/Documents ~/work
[jNf| /opt/local/lib/ruby/1.8 ]=>
```

In this example, I started in the ~/work directory, jumped over to the ~/Documents directory, and was then off to the Ruby install directory. Each time the *pushd* command is issued, it shows the existing directories already on the stack. This is true on all the Unix flavors I've tried. The Windows version of this command performs only the first two of the tasks above: it doesn't give you any clue of what's currently on the stack. However, this isn't a huge burden when using it, since this pair of commands is mostly used to make a quick jump to another place, then right back.

Command Prompts at Your Fingertips

Imagine yourself on the Productive Programmer therapy couch. "I'd really *like* to spend more time at the command line, but most of the stuff I need to do is in Explorer." Well, I'm here to help. A couple of ways exist to make it quick and easy to move back and forth between the graphical view and the command prompt.

Command Prompt Explorer Bar

NOTE
Embedded command prompts give you access to the best of both worlds.

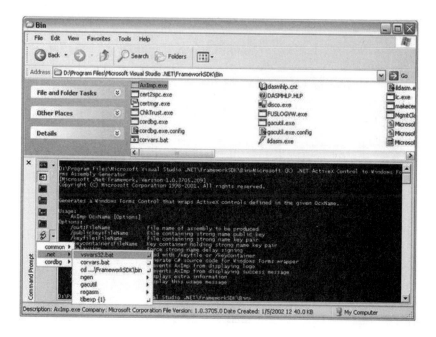

FIGURE 2-7. Command Prompt Explorer Bar

For Windows, Command Prompt Explorer Bar‡ is a great open source utility that allows you to open a command prompt attached to the bottom of your current Explorer view, using the keyboard shortcut Ctrl-M. See this utility in action in Figure 2-7. One of the great usability features of this tool is its "stickiness" for the directory shown in the attached Explorer view. When you change directories in Explorer, the directory automatically changes in the command prompt below. Unfortunately, the relationship isn't two-way: changing the directory in the command prompt window does not change it in the Explorer view. Nevertheless, it is a useful utility.

Unfortunately, Mac OS X doesn't have any native ability to perform this trick. However, the commercial Finder replacement Path Finder§ can make it happen, as shown in Figure 2-8. This terminal is like any other terminal window in Mac OS X (it reads your home profile, etc.), and it is launchable with the keyboard shortcut Alt-Apple-B. Once you become accustomed to having a terminal (or command prompt) so easily accessible, you tend to use it more for appropriate tasks.

The graphical view of the directory structure (Explorer, Finder) can also interact with the command-line view (command prompt, terminal) in a related but obscure way via drag-and-

‡ Download at *http://www.codeproject.com/csharp/CommandBar.asp*.

§ Download at *http://www.cocoatech.com/*.

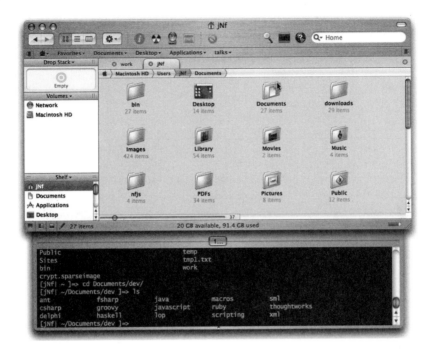

FIGURE 2-8. Path Finder's attached terminal

drop. In both Windows and Mac OS X, you can drag a directory into a command-line view to copy the path. Thus, if you want to change to a certain directory in the command prompt and you have Windows Explorer open to the parent folder (or anywhere that you can grab the target directory), type *cd* and then drag the directory to the command prompt and it will fill in the name of the directory. You can also use *Command Prompt Here*, discussed in the next section.

And one more cool trick in Mac OS X. If you go to Finder and copy files, you can access them in a terminal window by performing a paste operation (Apple-V); Mac OS X brings the whole path with the filename. You can also interact with the clipboard for piping operations using *pbcopy* (which copies stuff to the clipboard) and *pbpaste* (which pastes stuff from the clipboard to the command line). However, note that *pbpaste* just pastes the filename, not the entire path.

Here!

NOTE
Embed the command prompt with Explorer to make it easier to switch contexts.

I have one last entry in this family of acceleration tools. If you take the time and trouble to navigate the long, torturous route to get to a directory in Windows Explorer, you don't want to walk the same path again in a command prompt. Fortunately, one of the Microsoft PowerToys can come to your rescue: *Command Prompt Here*. Installing this PowerToy makes a few tweaks to the registry and adds a context (that is, right-click) menu called, as you can probably guess, "Command Prompt Here." Executing this command opens a command prompt in the directory you have selected.

POWERTOYS

Microsoft issues (but doesn't support) a collection of utilities known as PowerToys.[||] These power toys add all sorts of interesting capabilities to Windows, going all the way back to Windows 95, and they are all free. A lot of them (like Tweak UI) are really just dialogs that do special tweaks to registry entries. Some PowerToys include:

Tweak UI
> Allows you to control all sorts of visual aspects of Windows, like what icons appear on the desktop, mouse behaviors, and other hidden capabilities.

TaskSwitch
> Improved task switcher (tied to Alt-Tab, which shows thumbnails of the running applications).

Virtual Desktop Manager
> Virtual desktops for Windows (see "Segregate Your Workspace with Virtual Desktops" in Chapter 3).

Microsoft doesn't support these little utilities. If you've never played with them, go look at the list. Chances are pretty good that something you've always wanted Windows to do for you is already there.

Not to be outdone, you can obtain a *"Bash Here"* context menu by running *chere* from Cygwin, which opens a Cygwin bash shell at that location instead of a command prompt. These two tools play together nicely, so you can install both and decide on a case-by-case basis whether you want a command prompt or a bash shell. The command:

```
chere -i
```

installs the "Bash Here" context menu and:

```
chere -u -s bash
```

uninstalls it. Actually, the *chere* utility will also install a Windows command prompt "Command Prompt Here" context menu (just like the Windows PowerToy) via the command:

[||] Download at *http://www.microsoft.com/windowsxp/downloads/powertoys/xppowertoys.mspx*.

```
chere -i -s cmd
```

So, if you have Cygwin, there is no need to download the "Command Prompt Here" PowerToy, just use *chere*.

Path Finder in Mac OS X also has an "Open in Terminal" context menu option, which opens yet another terminal window (not the drawer version depicted in Figure 2-8 but a full-blown separate window). And Quicksilver has an action called "Go to the directory in Terminal."

Development Accelerators

Pop quiz: what's the biggest clickable target on your screen? It's the one right under your cursor, which is why the right-mouse menu should have the most important things on it. The target right under your mouse is effectively infinitely large. Second question: what's the next biggest target? The edges of the screen because you can accelerate as fast as possible to the edge and not overshoot it. This suggests that the really important stuff should reside on the edges of the screen. These observations come from Fitt's Law, which states that the ease of clicking on a target with the mouse is a combination of the distance you must navigate and the size of the target.

The designers of Mac OS X knew this law, which is why the menu bar resides at the top of the screen. When you use the mouse to click one of the menu items, you can ram the mouse pointer up against the top of the screen and you are where you want to be. Windows, on the other hand, has a title bar at the top of each window. Even if the window is maximized, you still must carefully find your target by accelerating to the top, and then use some precision mousing to hit the target.

There is a way to mitigate this for some Windows applications. The Microsoft Office suite has a "Full Screen" mode, which gets rid of the title bar and puts the menu right at the top, like Mac OS X. There is help for developers, too. Visual Studio features the same full-screen mode, as does IntelliJ for Java developers. If you are going to use the mouse, using your applications in full-screen mode makes it easier to hit the menus.

But speeding up the use of the mouse isn't really what I advocate. Programming (except for user interface design) is a text-based activity, so you should strive to keep your hands on the keyboard as much as possible.

> **NOTE**
> When coding, always prefer the keyboard to the mouse.

You use an IDE all day long to create code, and IDEs have a huge number of keyboard shortcuts. Learn them all! Using the keyboard to get around in source code is always faster than using a mouse. But the sheer number of keyboard shortcuts can be intimidating. The best way to learn them is to make a conscious effort to internalize them. Reading big lists isn't helpful because the shortcuts aren't in context. The Eclipse IDE has a nice shortcut key that shows all the other

```
34    }
35
36    public Object[] toArray() {
37        return _set.toArray();
38    }
```

⌘⇧⌥C (Copy Reference)

4 time(s)

```
public boolean add(Object o) {
    _count++;
    return _set.add(o);
}
```

FIGURE 2-9. Key Promoter is IntelliJ's useful nag about shortcuts

shortcut keys for a particular view: Ctrl-Shift-L. This is a great mnemonic because it's already in the appropriate context. The best time to learn keyboard shortcuts is when you need to perform the activity. When you go to the menu, notice the keyboard shortcut on it. Then, instead of selecting the menu item, remember the shortcut, dismiss the menu, and do it on the keyboard. That will reinforce the association between the task and the keyboard shortcut. And believe it or not, saying the shortcut aloud also helps because it forces it into more parts of your brain. Of course, your coworkers might think you're insane, but you'll be able to out-keyboard them in no time.

One of my colleagues has a great way of teaching keyboard shortcuts. Whenever you pair-program with him, if you use a mouse to select a menu or tool button, he makes you undo your operation, then do it three times using the keyboard. Yes, it slows you down at first, but the reinforcement (plus his evil eye when you forget them) is a pressure cooker to learn shortcuts.

> **NOTE**
> Learn IDE keyboard shortcuts in context, not by reading long lists.

Another great way to remember shortcuts is to have someone (or something) pester you about them. IntelliJ has an awesome plug-in called Key Promoter. Every time you use the menu to select something, a dialog pops up that tells you the shortcut you could have used and how many times you've done it wrong (see Figure 2-9). The same utility, called Key Prompter, exists for Eclipse as well.[#] Key Prompter goes even further: you can set a mode that will *ignore* menu selections, forcing you to use the shortcut key!

Unfortunately, lots of great shortcuts don't live on menu items at all: they are buried in the massively long list of possible keyboard shortcuts. You should ferret out the cool ones for the IDE you use. Table 2-1 is a short list for Java developers of some cool, hidden keyboard shortcuts in both IntelliJ and Eclipse for Windows.

[#] Download at *http://www.mousefeed.com*.

TABLE 2-1. Choice keyboard shortcuts for IntelliJ & Eclipse

Description	IntelliJ	Eclipse
Goto class	Ctrl-N	Ctrl-Shift-T
Symbol list	Alt-Ctrl-Shift-N	Ctrl-O
Incremental search	Alt-F3	Ctrl-J
Recently edited files/files open	Ctrl-E	Ctrl-E
Introduce variable	Ctrl-Alt-V	Alt-Shift-L
Escalating selection	Ctrl-W	Alt-Shift-Up Arrow

A couple of these entries require a little further explanation. The *recently edited files/files open* entry works differently across the two IDEs: in IntelliJ, it provides a list of files you've edited recently, in the reverse order of access (so that the most recent file is at the top). In Eclipse, the keyboard shortcut provides a list of open buffers. This is important to developers because we tend to work in a small clustering of files on a regular basis, so ready access to a small group helps.

Introduce variable is technically a refactoring function, but I use it constantly to type the lefthand side of expressions for me. In both IDEs, you can type the righthand side of an expression (such as `Calender.getInstance();`) and let the IDE supply the lefthand side (in this case, `Calendar calendar = `). The IDE can supply variable names almost as well as you can, and it's much less typing and thinking about what to name variables. (This shortcut has made me particularly lazy when coding in Java.)

The last special entry is *escalating selection*. Here's how it works. When you place your cursor on something and invoke this command, it extends the selection one level toward the next higher syntactic element. The next time you hit they key, it broadens the selection to the next larger group of syntactic elements. Because the IDE understands Java syntax, it knows what constitutes a token, a code block, a method, etc. Instead of creating a half-dozen shortcuts to select each of those elements, you can use the same keystroke over and over to gradually widen the selection. It's cumbersome to describe, but try it, you'll quickly fall in love.

Here is the way to learn *and internalize* the really cool keyboard shortcuts you saw in the Giant Long List of keyboard shortcuts. Read the list one more time, but copy the really useful ones you didn't know about to a separate file (or even paper!). Try to remember that the capability exists, and the next time you need it, look at your cheat sheet. This represents the missing link between "I know that it can be done" to "this is how to do it."

The other key to IDE productivity is *live templates*. These are snippets of code that represent some chunk of code you use all the time. Most IDEs allow you to parameterize your templates, filling in values when the template is expanded in your editor. For example, here is a parameterized template in IntelliJ that allows you to iterate over an array in Java:

```
for(int $INDEX$ = 0; $INDEX$ < $ARRAY$.length; $INDEX$++) {
    $ELEMENT_TYPE$ $VAR$ = $ARRAY$[$INDEX$];
```

```
    $END$
}
```

When this template is expanded, the IDE first places the cursor on the first $ delimited value, allowing you to type in your index name, then a tab takes you to the next parameter. In this template language, the END marker is where the cursor will end after all the expansions.

Every IDE has a different syntax for this, but virtually every IDE worth using supports this concept. Learn the template language in your IDE and use it as much as you can. Outstanding template support is one of the reasons for the popularity of the TextMate * and E-Text† editors. The template doesn't make typos, and having templates around for complex language constructs saves you time and mental energy while you code.

> NOTE
> When you type a complicated construct for the second time, templatize it.

Search Trumps Navigation in Tools, Too

Code hierarchies have also gotten too deep to be useful. Once they reach a certain size, filesystems, package structures, and other hierarchical systems become too deep for effective navigation. Large Java projects suffer from this because the package structure is tied to the directory structure. Even for a small project, you must dig through trees—expanding nodes as you go—to find a file, even if you already know the name of it. If you find yourself doing this, you are working too hard for your computer.

Modern Java IDEs allow you to quickly find any Java source files within the current project by typing Ctrl-N on Windows or Apple-N on the Mac (for IntelliJ) and Ctrl-Shift-T (for Eclipse). The example shown in Figure 2-10 is from IntelliJ; it opens a text box in the editor, allowing you to type the name of the file you want.

FIGURE 2-10. IntelliJ's "find files" text box

Typing in the entire name (or even a significant portion of it) is cumbersome. It would be nice if the IDE were even smarter about how you specify names. And it is. Instead of typing the name of the file, if you start typing capital letters, it looks for names that have that same pattern of capital letters. For example, if you are looking for the file *ShoppingCartMemento*, you can

---

* *Download at http://macromates.com/.*

† *Download at http://www.e-texteditor.com/.*

FIGURE 2-11. IntelliJ's smart pattern matching for names

type SCM and the IDE will ignore the intervening lowercase letters and find the matching pattern of capital letters, as shown in Figure 2-11.

This file-finding magic works with non-Java source files, too (add a Shift to the other keys in IntelliJ, or use Ctrl-Shift-R in Eclipse). This is the "find resources" textfield, and it works just like the "find files" one. Don't go slogging through the huge tree of source files anymore: you know what you want, so go directly to it.

For .NET developers, the common environment is Visual Studio 2005 (in its current incarnation). While it has a middling number of keyboard shortcuts, you can super-charge it with the commercial Resharper (from JetBrains, the creators of the IntelliJ Java IDE). Many developers think that Resharper concerns itself primarily with adding refactoring support, but savvy developers realize that it also adds a huge number of keyboard shortcuts (including the "find files" capability described earlier).

Macros

Macros are recorded snippets of interaction with your computer. Generally, each tool comes with its own macro recorder (because only the tool knows how it processes keys). That means, of course, that there is no standard macro syntax, sometimes even between different versions of a product. For years, Microsoft Word and Excel had very different macro syntax even though they were from the same company and in the same Office suite. It wasn't until Office 2000 that Microsoft finally agreed on a single syntax. Even though a Tower of Babel exists between tools, macros can still help solve very specific problems that you face on a daily basis.

Macro Recorder

> NOTE
> For any symmetric operation on multiple lines of text, find a pattern and record a macro.

How often do you find yourself working in a pattern? You've cut and pasted some information from an XML document, and now you have to remove all the XML cruft from around the real data inside to clean it up. Macros used to be all the rage with developers, but they seem to have fallen out of favor recently. I suspect that the live template feature of most modern IDEs has removed some of the need for macros.

But, however much you lean on live templates, uses still exist for recording macros. The common scenario is the one highlighted earlier: doing one-time processing on some information to either de-cruft it from another format or cruft it up for the consumption of some other tool. If you can shift your perspective on the task and see it as a series of repeatable steps, you'll find macros can be used for lots of chores.

> **NOTE**
> The more times you perform a particular operation on a chunk of text, the greater the likelihood you'll do it again.

Even if you use Eclipse (which doesn't have a macro recorder), you can always jump over to a text editor and use its macro recorder for just this chore. One of the important selection criteria for a text editor is its macro recording facilities and the format of the recorded macros. It is nicer if the macros produce some kind of readable code that you can tweak by hand, creating a reusable asset you can use later down the road. After all, if you've cut and pasted some stuff from one format to another once, chances are good you'll have to do it again.

Key Macro Tools

While formal macros in editors are great for processing text, code, and transformations, another category of macro tools helps you out on a daily basis. All the major operating systems have open source and/or commercial *key macro* tools. Key macro tools run in the background, waiting for a text pattern to expand. They allow you to type an abbreviation instead of the full text of something. Mostly, these tools do things like automatically type salutations for email addresses. But, as developers, we type lots of repetitive text in places where we don't have live templates (like the command line or in web browsers).

> **NOTE**
> Don't type the same commands over and over again.

One of the tasks I have to perform all the time is showing people how to use Selenium's remote control feature. To make it work, you must start up a proxy server and issue cryptic commands to give it instructions, which are basically just incantations at the command line. I'm not in an IDE, so I can't use live templates or even macros. I can't even use batch or shell scripts: I'm running against an interactive proxy. It didn't take me long to realize that I should save these commands in my key macro tool:

```
cmd=getNewBrowserSession&1=*firefox&2=8080
cmd=open&1=/art_emotherearth_memento/welcome&sessionId=
```

The ugly line of code is issued after I start the proxy server for Selenium, in the very particular format that Remote Control Selenium requires. If you don't know anything about Selenium, these commands won't make sense. But making sense out of the commands isn't the point of the example. This is just one of the hideous command strings that I must type from time to time. Every developer ends up with these, and they never make sense out of context (and frequently just barely when in context). But now, instead of copying and pasting this from somewhere, I just type *rcsl1* to generate the first line, *rcsl2* to generate the second, and so on for the 10 commands I need to show people.

Some key macro tools allow you to record keystrokes at the operating system–level and play them back (sometimes even capturing mouse clicks and other interactions). Others require you to type in the commands that you want associated with a particular macro. In both cases, you are capturing some operating system-level interaction that you have to do repeatedly in a format that makes it easy to reuse.

Key macro tools are also great for common phrases that you must type over and over. What about the text you have to type in Word for project status messages? Or entering hours in your time and expenses system? A key macro tool falls into the category of tools that you don't even know exists one day into the "how did I live without this?" category the next.

The most popular key macro tool for Windows is AutoHotKey[‡] (which is open source). Mac OS X has a couple in the "commercial but inexpensive category," like TextExpander[§] and Typinator.[||]

Summary

It's one thing to talk about accelerating your computer interactions with launchers, clipboard managers, IDE shortcuts, and all the various things mentioned in this chapter. It's another to *apply* them. You know what speeds up your work, but you feel like you don't have time to apply it. "I know there's a keyboard shortcut that does this, but I'm in a hurry, so I'll use the mouse instead and look up that keyboard shortcut later." Later never comes. Becoming more productive involves finding a balance between pursuing productivity without gutting your current productivity (I know, this drips with irony). Try to tackle one productivity enhancer per week, concentrate on just that one until it becomes ingrained, then move on to the next. This method will have very little impact on your time, and you'll gradually accrue better productivity.

> NOTE
> Spend a little time each day to make every day more productive.

Applying acceleration has two contexts: knowledge of accelerators and the proper context in which to use them. For example, install a clipboard utility on your machine and force yourself

[‡] Download at *http://www.autohotkey.com/*.

[§] Download at *http://www.smileonmymac.com/textexpander/index.html*.

[||] Download at *http://www.ergonis.com/products/typinator/*.

to think about it every time you need to copy and paste something. You will gradually start seeing situations where it saves you time because you are harvesting a set of copied values all at once, then pasting them as a group as well. Once you've internalized that utility, move on to another one. It's all about finding the balance of spending time to learn to become more productive.

CHAPTER THREE

Focus

THIS CHAPTER INTRODUCES A VARIETY OF WAYS TO ENHANCE YOUR FOCUS BY KILLING OFF inefficiencies and needless distractions. You probably suffer from lots of distractions at work, both from the computer itself and from the outside world. Here you will learn how to enhance your focus with specific tools and approaches to interacting with your computer, as well as ways to make your coworkers leave you alone so that you can quit banging rocks together and get some work done. The goal is to get you back to that dazed but happy state of just having scaled a virtual mountain.

Kill Distractions

You are a knowledge worker, meaning you are paid for the creative and innovative ideas you produce. Dealing with constant distractions, both at your desk and on your desktop, can threaten your best contributions to your projects. Developers crave a state known as *flow*, discussed in lots of places (it even has an entire book devoted to it, written by Csikszentmihalyi). All developers know this state: it's when you are so focused that time disappears, you develop an almost symbiotic relationship with the machine and the problem you are attacking. This is the state you've been in when you say, "Wow, have four hours passed? I didn't even notice." The problem with flow is that it is fragile. One distraction pulls you out, and it takes effort to get back in. It also suffers from inertia. Late in the day, you have to fight harder to get back to that state, and the more times you are abruptly pulled out, the harder it becomes. Distractions kill your focus on the problem at hand, making you less productive. Fortunately, you can effectively block distractions in a few simple ways.

> NOTE
> The higher the level of concentration, the denser the ideas.

Blocking Strategies

Concentration is hard to maintain, especially when your computer seems determined to drag your attention away from your work. Blocking visual and audible distractions helps you maintain a good, focused flow state. For audible distractions (especially if you don't have an office with a door you can close), you can wear headphones (even if you aren't listening to music). When others see you wearing headphones, they are less likely to interrupt you. If your office won't allow headphones, consider putting a "Do Not Disturb" sign on the entryway to your cubicle. That should make people think twice before barging in.

For visual distractions, turn off all the things on your machine that break your concentration. Email notification is very damaging because it creates artificial urgency. How many of the emails you receive in the course of a day really require an immediate response? Turn off your email client and check mail in batches, when you reach a natural breaking point in your work. This allows you to determine when you want to break your train of thought.

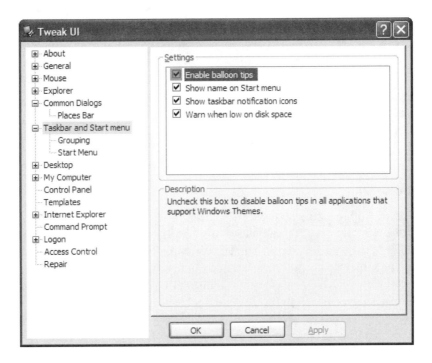

FIGURE 3-1. Killing balloon tips with Tweak UI

Turn Off Needless Notifications

Balloon tips in Windows and Growl notifications on Mac OS X also drag your attention away. On Mac OS X, Growl is customizable, so you can turn on only the notifications you need to see to get work done. Unfortunately, balloon tips in Windows are all-or-nothing. And lots of the messages balloon tips deliver are not useful. Do you really want to stop working to clean up the unused icons on your desktop? You also get messages about Windows automatically resizing virtual memory. I don't want to know that, and I especially don't want to be interrupted from my work to see it. Windows sometimes seems like a spoiled three-year old, always clamoring for attention.

There are two ways to turn off balloon tips. If you already have the Tweak UI PowerToy, one of the settings disables balloon tips, as shown in Figure 3-1. The other way involves a little registry editing (which is all the PowerToy is doing behind the scenes):

1. Run regedit.

2. Look for *HKEY_CURRENT_USER \Software\Microsoft\Windows\CurrentVersion \Explorer\Advanced*.

3. Create a DWORD value (or edit it if it already exists) named EnableBalloonTips with value 0.

4. Log off and log in again.

If you tend to create lots of overlapping windows when you work, these can become distracting as well. There are a couple of freeware utilities available that are designed to "black out" the background, making all the applications you are not using fade out. This keeps your focus tightly bound to the task at hand.

For Windows, the application JediConcentrate[*] does the job. For Mac OS X, the fadeout application is called Doodim.[†] They both work the same way, allowing you to customize how much you want the background dimmed.

Create Quiet Time

If you work in an office with lots of other developers, consider instituting "quiet time," for example, from 9 A.M. to 11 A.M. and 3 P.M. to 5 P.M. During this time, everyone has their email turned off, there are no meetings, and it is verboten to call or go talk to someone unless there is an emergency (like you are blocked and can't get work done on the problem you are trying to solve). I tried this in one of the consulting offices where I worked, and it had an amazing outcome. Everyone in the office found that we got more done in those four hours than we were getting done in an entire day before we implemented the policy. All the developers started looking forward to it; it was everyone's favorite time of the day.

Another development team I know periodically books a meeting in their shared calendar. The "meeting" is really just time to get stuff done. Other people at the company can see from the shared calendar that everyone is "meeting" and therefore know not to disturb them. It is tragic that office environments so hamper productivity that employees have to game the system to get work done. Sometimes you have to think outside the box (or cubicle) to get work done despite your environment.

Search Trumps Navigation

NOTE
The bigger the haystack, the harder it is to find the needle.

Projects have gotten bigger and bigger, along with the packages and namespaces that go along with them. Hierarchies are hard to navigate when they get big: they're too deep. Filesystems that work well with 200 MB of storage suffer when they reach 200 GB. Filesystems have become massive haystacks, and we constantly do hard target searches for needles. Taking time out to dig around for files pulls you away from the problem upon which you should be focusing.

[*] Download at *http://www.gyrolabs.com/2006/09/25/jediconcentrate-mod/*.

[†] Download at *http://www.lachoseinteractive.net/en/products/doodim/*.

Fortunately, new search tools help you dispense with cumbersome filesystem navigation almost entirely.

Recently, powerful search applications appeared at the operating system–level: Spotlight in Mac OS X and Windows Search in Vista. These searching applications are different from the quaint search features in previous versions of Windows (whose only real use was to show an animation of a dog). This new breed of search tools indexes the interesting parts of your entire hard drive, making searches blazingly fast. They don't just look at filenames: they index the contents of files.

Several desktop search add-ons exist for pre-Vista Windows. My current favorite is the free Google Desktop Search.[‡] Out of the box, it searches only "normal" files (like spreadsheets, Word documents, email, etc.). One of the best parts of Google Desktop Search is its plug-in API, which allows developers to add search plug-ins. For example, Larry's Any Text File Indexer[§] allows you to configure Google Desktop Search for source files.

Once you've installed Larry's Any Text File Indexer and allowed it to index your hard drive (which it does in the background, during idle times), you can search for a snippet of the *contents* of a file. For example, in Java, the name of the file must match the name of the public class. In most other languages (like C#, Ruby, Python), the filename conventionally matches the class name. Or, if you are looking for all the files that use a particular class, you can search for code fragments you know exist. For example:

```
new OrderDb();
```

finds all the classes that create an instance of your OrderDb class.

Searching by contents is extremely powerful. Even if you can't remember the exact name of a file, you can almost always remember at least some of the content.

> **NOTE**
> Replace file hierarchies with search.

Indexing search utilities free you from the tyranny of the filesystem. Using a search tool like Google Desktop Search takes acclimatization because you likely have well-worn habits of searching for files by hand. You don't need this level of search for retrieving source files (your IDE already handles that for you). However, you constantly need to access a file where it lives, to perform some operation on it like version control, a diff, or refering to something from a different project. Google Desktop Search allows you to right-click on the found file and open the containing folder.

[‡] Download at *http://desktop.google.com*.

[§] Download at *http://desktop.google.com/plugins/i/indexitall.html*.

Spotlight in Mac OS X lets you do the same thing. When you find a file, if you hit Enter, it opens the file in the associated application. If you hit Apple-Enter, it opens the enclosing folder. Just as with Google Desktop Search, you can download Spotlight plug-ins that allow it to index your source files. For example, you can download a Spotlight plug-in from the Apple site to add Ruby code as an index target.‖

Spotlight now allows you to add search filters to your searches. For example, you can add *kind:email* to your search string and Spotlight will restrict its search to only emails. This harkens to the near future of searching, the ability to search via customizable attributes (see the next sidebar "The Near Future: Search Via Attributes").

THE NEAR FUTURE: SEARCH VIA ATTRIBUTES

Searching for files by title alone isn't that useful. Remembering the exact title is just as impossible as remembering where you put it. Searching by content is better because you are more likely to remember at least part of the file.

An even more powerful variant is coming to leading-edge software: the ability to search for files based on customizable attributes. For example, let's say you have some files that belong to the same project: Java source files, SQL schema, project notes, and tracking spreadsheets. Putting these items together in the file hierarchy makes some sense because they all relate to the same project. But what if some of the files need to be shared between several projects? Search allows you to find them based on the things in which they participate, not on their physical locations.

Eventually, we'll get filesystems that "understand" the idea that you can tag files with arbitrary attributes. You can do that now in Mac OS X using Spotlight Comments, which allows you to tag the files that belong to the same logical project without worrying about their physical location. Windows Vista also offers a similar feature. If your operating system offers this feature, use it! It is a much better way to organize your groups of files.

Find Hard Targets

> **NOTE**
> Try simple searching before resorting to "hard target" searching.

Google Desktop Search, Spotlight, and Vista's search are great for finding files when you know some of the content. But sometimes you want more sophisticated searching capabilities. None of the aforementioned tools supports regular expressions, which is a shame because regular

‖ Download at *http://www.apple.com/downloads/macosx/spotlight/rubyimporter.html.*

expressions have been around a long time and offer an incredibly powerful search mechanism. The more efficiently you can find something, the sooner you can return your focus to the problem at hand.

All flavors of Unix (including Mac OS X, Linux, and even Cygwin in Windows) include a utility called *find*. Find is responsible for finding files from the given directory downward, recursing through directory structures. Find takes tons of parameters that allow you to refine your searches, including regular expressions for filenames. For example, here is a *find* invocation that locates all Java sources files with "Db" right before the file extension:

```
find . -regex ".*Db\.java"
```

This search tells *find* to start from the current directory (the ".") and find all files that have zero or more characters (the ".*") before the string "Db", which comes before the "." (which must be escaped because "." normally means "any single character"), followed by the file extension of Java.

find is pretty darn useful by itself, but when you combine it with *grep*, you have a really powerful team. One of the options on *find* is *-exec*, which executes the command(s) that follow with the option of passing the found filename as a parameter. In other words, *find* will find all the files that match your criteria and then pass each file (as it's discovered) to the command to the right of *-exec*. Consider this command (explained in Table 3-1):

```
find . -name "*.java" -exec grep -n -H "new .*Db.*" {} \;
```

TABLE 3-1. Decoding the find command

Character(s)	What it's doing
find	Execute the *find* command.
.	From the current directory.
-name	Match the name of "*.java" (note that this isn't a regular expression, it's a filesystem "glob," where the * means all matches).
-exec	Execute the following command on each found file.
grep	*grep* command, the powerful *-nix utility used for searching for strings within files.
-n	Show line numbers of the matches.
-H	Show filenames of the matches.
"new .*Db.*"	Match the regular expression that states "all files with any number of characters, followed by the letters Db, then followed by any characters."
{}	Placeholder for the filename found by *find*.
\;	Terminate the command after -exec. Because this is a Unix command, you might want to pipe the results of this into another command, and the *find* command has to know when the "exec" is done.

Although this is a lot of work, you can see the power of this combination of commands (for two different but equivalent versions of this particular combination of commands, check out "The Command Line" in Appendix A). Once you learn the syntax, you can literally query your code base. Here is another, slightly more complex example:

```
find -name "*.java" -not -regex ".*Db\.java" -exec grep -H -n "new .*Db" {} \;
```

You can use this combination of *find* + *grep* during code reviews, in fact, this example comes from a query I did during a code review. We were writing an application that adheres to the typical layered application design, with a model, a controller, and a view layer. All the classes that accessed the database ended with "Db", and the rule was that you shouldn't construct those classes except in controllers. Issuing the *find* command allowed me to find out exactly where all the boundary classes were being constructed and nip the problem in the bud before someone did something wrong.

Here's another little command-line trick for finding stuff. What if you want to go to the directory where some application that's on your path lives? For example, say you want to temporarily go to the directory where the executable command *java* lives. You can do so with a combination of the *pushd* and *which* commands:

```
pushd `which java`/..
```

Remember, any command in backticks (the `character) executes before the rest of the command. In this case, the *which* command (which finds the location of applications on your path) finds where *java* lives. But *java* is an application, not a directory. Thus, we take that location and back up to the parent, *pushd*-ing to it. This is a great example of the *composability* of *-nix commands.

Use Rooted Views

A r*ooted view* is a view of a directory structure rooted at a particular subdirectory, where you see only the contents from the root directory downward. If you are working on a particular project, you don't care about the files from other projects. Rooted views allow you to eliminate the distraction of out-of-context files and focus just on the set of files upon which you need to work right now. All the major platforms support this concept, but the implementations are different.

Rooted Views in Windows

A rooted Explorer view ("rooted" on the *c:\work\sample code\art \art_emotherearth_memento* folder) appears in Figure 3-2.

This is a normal Explorer window, opened with the following parameters:

```
explorer /e,/root,c:\work\cit
```

The rooted view affects only this instance of Explorer. If you launch another Explorer window using typical means, you'll see a normal instance of Explorer. To take advantage of rooted views, create shortcuts to Explorer with the rooted view parameters above. Rooted views work in all versions of Windows, from Windows 95 through Windows Vista.

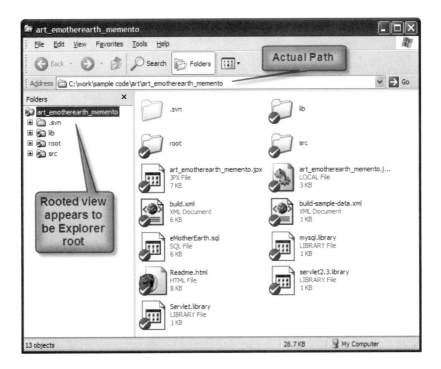

FIGURE 3-2. Rooted views in Windows

NOTE
Rooted views turn Explorer into a project management tool.

Rooted views are particularly good for project work and especially good if you use a file- or folder-based version control system (like Subversion or CVS). As far as the rooted instance of Explorer is concerned, your project files and folders make up the entire universe. You can access the plug-in Tortoise[#] (a Subversion management tool for Explorer) via any place you click within the rooted view. And, more importantly, you eliminate the distractions created by a bunch of folders and files that mean nothing to the project on which you are working.

Rooted Views in OS X

Root views work a little differently in Mac OS X. While you can't create a Finder view that is uniquely focused on a single directory structure like you can with Windows Explorer, you can still create specialized rooted views that cut through the massive directory structures. In Finder, you can create shortcuts to directories by dragging the directory in question to the sidebar or to the dock. This allows you to open that directory right from Finder, as shown in Figure 3-3.

[#] Download at *http://tortoisesvn.tigris.org/*.

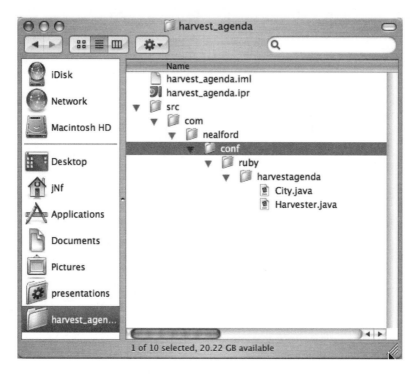

FIGURE 3-3. Rooted views in Finder

Use Sticky Attributes

The command line in Windows has a nasty surprise turned on by default called Quick Edit Mode. This is a switch set in the properties of the command window that allows you to select text to copy with the mouse. Any click inside the window starts a drag operation, highlighting a rectangular section of text, ready to copy it to the clipboard (oddly enough, the standard keyboard shortcut Ctrl-C doesn't work here; you have to hit the Enter key instead). Therein lies the problem. Because you are selecting text in the console window, it freezes all activity (that is, all the processes and threads occupying that window) as soon as you start dragging the mouse. This makes sense: it would be annoying to try to copy something that actively scrolls out of your way. Typically, in a windowed environment, it is perfectly safe to click anywhere in a window to give it focus. But if you click in a command prompt window, you've inadvertently started a drag operation, which freezes all the processes. Ironically, setting focus to a window can accidentally destroy the focus on the job at hand because you start wondering "Why is nothing happening in that window?" You can fix this "feature" using *sticky attributes*.

Windows keeps track of customized settings in command prompts via the title of the window. When you close a command prompt in Windows, it asks if you want to save these settings for all command prompts with the same title (thus making them "sticky"). You can leverage that to create specialized command prompts. Create a shortcut to launch a window with a specific title, set some options, and save the options for the window as you close it. For development work, you need a command prompt with the following characteristics:

- Almost infinite scrolling. The default is a measly 300 lines, which will easily scroll off when doing something interesting. Set it to 9999 lines (and ignore the 1990s-era warning that your command prompt will now eat a precious 2 MB of memory).

- The widest width that your screen will support without horizontal scrolling. Reading wrapped lines in a command prompt is tedious and error prone.

- Set the position. If this is a command window with a single purpose (like a servlet engine or Ant/Nant/Rake window), have it always appear in a known location. You will learn that location quickly, allowing you to know what this command prompt does without even looking at it.

- Set unique foreground and background colors. For common command prompts (like servlet engines), the color becomes an important clue as to the purpose of the window. You can quickly identify that a cyan background with yellow text is a Tomcat window, while a blue background with green text is a MySQL prompt window. When you cycle through open command prompts, the color (and position) tell you the purpose of this window faster than you can read.

- And, of course, turn off Quick Edit Mode.

Use Project-Based Shortcuts

All the major operating systems have some alias, link, or shortcut mechanism. Use it to create project management workspaces. Frequently, you have projects that have documents strewn all over your hard drive: requirements/use cases/story cards in one place, source code in another, database definitions in another. Navigating between all those folders is a waste of time. Instead of forcing all your files for a project into a single location, you can put them all together virtually. Make one project-based folder that has shortcuts and links for the entire project. You'll find that you spend much less time spelunking around the filesystem.

Place your project management folder under one of the Quick Launch buttons in Windows or on the dock in Mac OS X. These two areas don't support a large number of items, but using them for just a few project consolidator folders makes sense.

Multiply Your Monitors

Monitors have gotten cheap, and developers can use the extra real estate. It is penny-wise and dollar foolish not to supply developers with ultra-fast computers and dual monitors. Every moment that a knowledge worker stares at an hourglass is pure wasted productivity. Having to work to manage all the overlapping windows on a cramped monitor also wastes time.

Multiple monitors allow you to write code on one and debug on the other. Or keep documentation alongside your coding. Having multiple monitors is just the first step, though, because you can also segregate your dual workspaces into a bunch of specialized views using virtual desktops.

Segregate Your Workspace with Virtual Desktops

> NOTE
> Virtual desktops unclutter your stacks of windows.

One of the cool features from the Unix world is *virtual desktops*. A virtual desktop is just like your regular desktop, with windows in a certain arrangement, but the "virtual" part indicates that you can have more than one. Instead of having one massively jumbled desktop with your IDE, your database console, and all your email, instant messaging, browsers, etc. on it, you can have singly purposed desktops for each logical grouping of activities. A massive pile of windows on your desktop distracts you from your focus because you constantly have to sort through the windows.

Virtual desktops used to exist solely on high-end Unix workstations (which had the graphical horsepower to support such a thing). But now they exist on all the major platforms. On Linux, both GNOME and KDE have virtual desktops built-in.

The Leopard version of Mac OS X (version 10.5) added this feature, called Spaces. But previous Mac OS X users aren't left out: several open source and commercial virtual desktops exist, such as VirtueDesktops.[*] It offers sophisticated features such as "pinning" applications to a certain desktop (meaning that application will appear only on that desktop, and the focus will change to that desktop if you select that application). This is a great feature for developers, who typically set up certain desktops for specific purposes (development, documentation, debugging, etc.).

---

[*] Download at *http://virtuedesktops.info/*.

FIGURE 3-4. Managing desktops with Virtual Desktop Manager

One of my recent projects was a Ruby on Rails gig where we were pair-programming on Mac Minis (the little smaller-than-a-breadbox machines that you buy without a monitor or keyboard). They make surprisingly good development machines, especially with two keyboards, mice, and monitors. What made them great environments, though, were the virtual desktops. We had each machine set up the same way (to preserve sanity as we swapped pairs), with all the development tools on one desktop, documentation on another, and the running application (a terminal window running the web server in debug mode and browser) on a third. Each desktop was completely self-contained, and as we switched applications, the appropriate desktop rotated into view. The environment allowed us to leave all the windows for a particular desktop in the same place all the time, with very little tiling and cascading. In my last gig, I was coding alone on Windows, but I still set up "communication," "documentation," and "development" desktops, which cut down on clutter and aided my sanity.

Windows has a PowerToy called Virtual Desktop Manager to enable virtual desktops in Windows 2000 and Windows XP (see Figure 3-4). It allows you to manage up to four virtual desktops, each with a taskbar controller, unique wallpapers, and hotkey support. A virtual desktop isn't really a fundamental change to the underlying operating system; it's simply managing the appearance and state of the various windows behind the scenes.

Virtual desktops provide an excellent way to manage your concentration. They give you just the information or tool you need, at just the time you need it, without extraneous details. I tend to create virtual desktops opportunistically, depending on the type of work I'm doing. One of the nice features of both Spaces and the Virtual Desktop Manager is the ability to get an overview of your desktops. When I have a discrete task upon which I need to work, I launch the applications I need for it and move them all to a single desktop. That way, I can work on the project in isolation from all the other stuff that's also running on my machine. In fact, this chapter is being written on Desktop 2 as I type!

Summary

This chapter covered several different aspects of focus: finding ways to modify your environment to reduce distractions, ways to make your computer less distracting, and tools to enhance your focus. Hopefully, you can now see why I decided to organize the topics around the ideas of productivity principles: these topics would seem unrelated to one another without the unifying element of focus.

Focus in modern environments is hard to achieve. Yet, to fully realize your potential, you must find a way within your specific circumstances to carve out a workable space and environment. Doing so will ultimately greatly enhance your productivity.

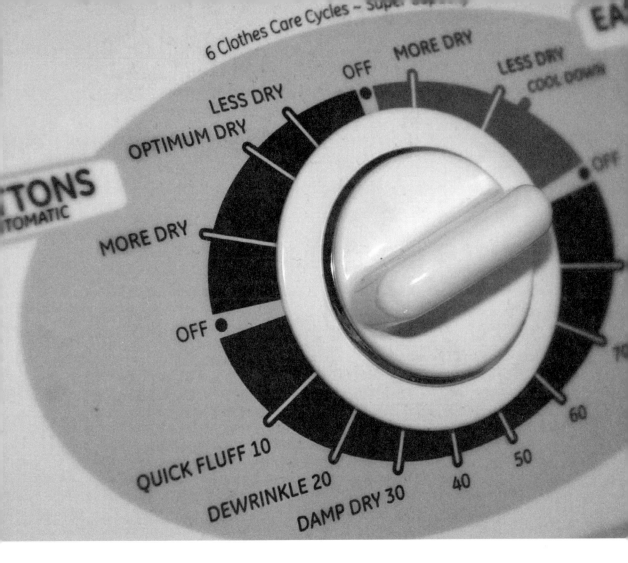

CHAPTER FOUR

Automation

I WAS WORKING ON A PROJECT THAT REQUIRED UPDATING SEVERAL SPREADSHEETS ON A
regular basis. I wanted to open Excel with multiple worksheets, but doing it by hand was
cumbersome (and Excel doesn't allow you to pass multiple files on a command line). So, I took
a few minutes to write the following little Ruby script:

```ruby
class DailyLogs
    private
    @@Home_Dir = "c:\\MyDocuments\\Documents\\"

  def doc_list
    docs = Array.new
    docs << "Sisyphus Project Planner.xls"
    docs << "TimeLog.xls"
    docs << "NFR.xls"
  end

  def open_daily_logs
    excel = WIN32OLE.new("excel.application")

    workbooks = excel.WorkBooks
    excel.Visible = true
    doc_list.each do |f|
      begin
        workbooks.Open(@@Home_Dir + f, true)
      rescue
        puts "Cannot open workbook:", @@Home_Dir + f
      end
    end
    excel.Windows.Arrange(7)
  end
end
DailyLogs.daily_logs
```

Even though it didn't take long to open the files by hand, the little time it took was still a waste
of time, so I automated it. Along the way, I discovered that you can use Ruby on Windows to
drive COM objects, like Excel.

Computers are designed to perform simple, repetitive tasks over and over really fast. Yet an
odd thing is happening: people are performing simple, repetitive tasks by hand on computers.
And the computers get together late at night and make fun of their users. How did this happen?

Graphical environments are designed to help novices. Microsoft created the Start button in
Windows because users had a hard time in previous versions knowing what to do first. (Oddly,
you also shut down the computer with the Start button.) But the very things that make casual
users more productive can hamper power users. You can get more done at the command line
for most development chores than you can through a graphical user interface. One of the great
ironies of the last couple of decades is that power users have gotten slower at performing
routine tasks. The typical Unix guys of yore were much more efficient because they automated
everything.

If you've ever been to an experienced woodworker's shop, you've seen lots of specialized tools
lying around (you may not have even realized that a laser-guided, gyroscopically balanced
lathe existed). Yet in the course of most projects, woodworkers use a little scrap of wood from

the floor to temporarily hold two things apart or hold two things together. In engineering terms, these little scraps are "jigs" or "shims." As developers, we create too few of these little throwaway tools, frequently, because, we don't think of tools in this way.

Software development has lots of obvious automation targets: builds, continuous integration, and documentation. This chapter covers some less obvious but no less valuable ways to automate development chores, from the single keystroke all the way to little applications.

Don't Reinvent Wheels

General infrastructure setup is something you have to do for every project: setting up version control, continuous integration, user IDs, etc. Buildix* is an open source project (developed by ThoughtWorks) that greatly simplifies this process for Java-based projects. Many Linux distributions come with a "Live CD" option, allowing you to try out a version of Linux right off the CD. Buildix works the same way, but with preconfigured project infrastructure. It is itself an Ubuntu Live CD, but with software development goodies preinstalled. Buildix includes the following preconfigured infrastructure:

- Subversion, the popular open source version control package
- CruiseControl, an open source continuous integration server
- Trac, open source bug tracking and wiki
- Mingle, ThoughtWorks' agile project tracking tool

You boot from the Buildix CD and you have project infrastructure. Or, you can use the Live CD as an installation CD for an existing Ubuntu system. It's a project in a box.

Cache Stuff Locally

When you develop software, you constantly refer to resources on the Internet. No matter how fast your network connection, you still pay a speed penalty when you view pages via the Web. For oft-referenced material (like programming APIs), you should cache the content locally (which also lets you access it on airplanes). Some content is easy to cache locally: just use your browser's "Save Page" feature. Lots of times, however, caching gets an incomplete set of web pages.

wget is a *-nix utility designed to cache parts of the web locally. It is available on all the *-nixes and as part of Cygwin on Windows. *wget* has lots of options to fetch pages. The most common is *mirror*, which mirrors the entire site locally. For example, to effectively mirror a web site, issue the following command:

```
wget --mirror â~@~Sw 2 --html-extension â~@~S-convert-links
     â~@~SP c:\wget_files\example1
```

---

* Download at *http://buildix.thoughtworks.com/*.

That's a mouthful. Table 4-1 gives a breakdown.

TABLE 4-1. Using the wget command

Character(s)	What it's doing
wget	The command itself.
--mirror	The command to mirror the web site. *wget* will recursively follow links on the site and download all necessary files. By default, it only gets files that were updated since the last mirror operation to avoid useless work.
--html-extension	Lots of web files have non-HTML extensions even if they ultimately yield HTML files (like cgi or PHP). This flag tells *wget* to convert those files to HTML extensions.
--convert-links	All links on the page are converted to local links, fixing the problem for a page that has absolute URIs in them. *wget* converts all the links to local resources.
-P c:\wget_files \example1	The target directory where you want the site placed locally.

Automate Your Interaction with Web Sites

There may be web sites from which you would like to distill information that require logon or other steps to get to content. cURL allows you to automate that interaction. cURL is another open source tool that is available for all the major operating systems. It is similar to *wget* but specializes in interacting with pages to retrieve content or grab resources. For example, say you have the following web form:

```
<form method="GET" action="junk.cgi">
        <input type=text name="birthyear">
        <input type=submit name=press value="OK">
</form>
```

cURL allows you to fetch the page that results after supplying the two parameters:

```
curl "www.hotmail.com/when/junk.cgi?birthyear=1905&press=OK"
```

You can also interact with pages that require an HTML POST instead of GET using the "-d" command-line option:

```
curl -d "birthyear=1905&press=%20OK%20" www.hotmail.com/when/junk.cgi
```

cURL's real sweet spot is interacting with secured sites via a variety of protocols (like HTTPS). The cURL web site goes into incredible detail on this subject. This ability to navigate security protocols and other web realities makes cURL a great tool to interact with sites. It comes by default on Mac OS X and most Linux distributions; you can download a copy for Windows at *http://www.curl.org*.

Interact with RSS Feeds

Yahoo! has a service (currently and perpetually in beta) called Pipes. The Pipes service allows you to manipulate RSS feeds (like blogs), combining, filtering, and processing the results to

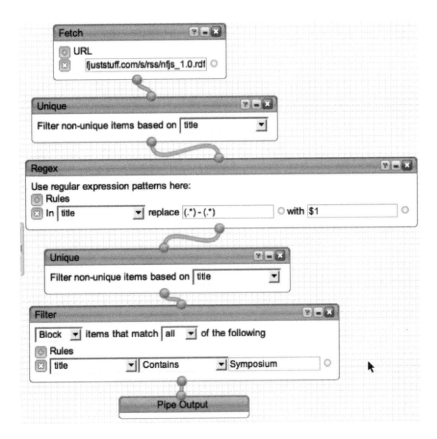

FIGURE 4-1. Regex pipes in action

create either a web page result or another RSS feed. It uses a web-based drag-and-drop interface to create "pipes" from one feed to another, borrowing the Unix command-line pipe metaphor. From a usability standpoint, it looks much like Mac OS X Automator, where each of the commands (or pipe stages) produces output to be consumed by the next pipe in line.

For example, the pipe shown in Figure 4-1 fetches the blog aggregator from the No Fluff, Just Stuff conference site that includes recent blog postings. The blog postings occur in the form of "blog author - blog title," but I want only the author in the output, so I use the regex pipe to replace the author-title with just the author's name.

The output of the pipe is either another HTML page or another RSS feed (the pipe is executed whenever you refresh the feed).

RSS is an increasingly popular format for developer information, and Yahoo! Pipes allows you to programmatically manipulate it to refine the results. Not only that, Pipes is gradually adding support for harvesting information off web pages to put into pipes, allowing you to automate retrieval of all sorts of web-based information.

Subvert Ant for Non-Build Tasks

NOTE
Use tools out of their original context when appropriate.

Batch files and bash scripts allow you to automate work at the operating system–level. But both have picky syntax and sometimes clumsy commands. For example, if you need to perform an operation on a large number of files, it is difficult to retrieve just the list of files you want using the primitive commands in batch files and bash scripts. Why not use tools already designed for this purpose?

The typical make commands we use now as development tools already know how to grab lists of files, filter them, and perform operations on them. Ant, Nant, and Rake have much friendlier syntax than batch and script files for tasks that must operate on groups of files.

Here is an example of subverting Ant to do some work that would be so difficult in a batch file that I never would have bothered. I used to teach a lot of programming classes where I wrote samples on the fly. Frequently, because of questions, I would customize the application as we went along. At the end of the week, everyone wanted a copy of the custom applications I had written. But in the course of writing them, lots of extra stuff piled up (output files, JAR files, temporary files, etc.), so I had to clean out all of the extraneous files and create a nice ZIP archive for them. Rather than doing this by hand, I created an Ant file do to it. The nice part about using Ant was a built-in awareness of a set of files:

```
<target name="clean-all" depends="init">
    <delete verbose="true" includeEmptyDirs="true">
    <fileset dir="${clean.dir}">
        <include name="**/*.war" />
        <include name="**/*.ear" />
        <include name="**/*.jar" />
        <include name="**/*.scc" />
        <include name="**/vssver.scc" />
        <include name="**/*.*~" />
        <include name="**/*.~*~" />
        <include name="**/*.ser" />
        <include name="**/*.class" />
        <containsregexp expression=".*~$" />
    </fileset>
    </delete>

    <delete verbose="true" includeEmptyDirs="true" >
        <fileset dir="${clean.dir}" defaultexcludes="no">
            <patternset refid="generated-dirs" />
        </fileset>
    </delete>
</target>
```

Using Ant allowed me to write a high-level task to perform all the steps I was doing by hand before:

```
<target name="zip-samples" depends="clean-all" >
    <delete file="${class-zip-name}" />
```

```
        <echo message="Your file name is ${class-zip-name}" />
        <zip destfile="${class-zip-name}.zip" basedir="." compress="true" excludes="*.xml,*.zip, *.cmd" />
    </target>
```

Writing this as a batch file would have been a nightmare! Even writing it in Java would be cumbersome: Java has no built-in awareness of a set of files matching patterns. When using build tools, you don't have to create a `main` method or any of the other infrastructure already supplied by the build tools.

The worst thing about Ant is its reliance on XML, which is hard to write, hard to read, hard to refactor, and hard to diff. A nice alternative is Gant.[†] It provides the ability to interact with existing Ant tasks, but you write your build files in Groovy, meaning that you are now in a real programming language.

Subvert Rake for Common Tasks

Rake is the make utility for Ruby (written in Ruby). Rake makes a great shell script substitute because it gives you the full expressive power of Ruby but allows you to easily interact with the operating system.

Here's an example that I use all the time. I do lots of presentations at developers' conferences, which means that I have lots of slide decks and corresponding example code. For a long time, I would launch the presentation, then remember all the other tools and samples I would have to launch. Inevitably, I would forget one and have to fumble around during the talk to find the missing sample. Then I wised up and automated the process:

```
require File.dirname(__FILE__) + '/../base'
TARGET = File.dirname(__FILE__)

FILES = [
  "#{PRESENTATIONS}/building_dsls.key",
  "#{DEV}/java/intellij/conf_dsl_builder/conf_dsl_builder.ipr",
  "#{DEV}/java/intellij/conf_dsl_logging/conf_dsl_logging.ipr",
  "#{DEV}/java/intellij/conf_dsl_calendar_stopping/conf_dsl_calendar_stopping.ipr",
  "#{DEV}/thoughtworks/rbs/intarch/common/common.ipr"
]

APPS = [
  "#{TEXTMATE} #{GROOVY}/dsls/",
  "#{TEXTMATE} #{RUBY}/conf_dsl_calendar/",
  "#{TEXTMATE} #{RUBY}/conf_dsl_context"
]
```

This rake file lists all the files that I need to open and all the applications required for the talk. One of the nice things about Rake is its ability to use Ruby files as helpers. This rake file is essentially just declarations. The actual work is done in a base rake file called *base*, which all the individual rake files rely upon.

```
require 'rake'
require File.dirname(__FILE__) + '/locations'
```

---

† Download at *http://gant.codehaus.org/*.

```
require File.dirname(__FILE__) + '/talks_helper'

task :open do
  TalksHelper.new(FILES, APPS).open_everything
end
```

Notice at the top of the file I require a file named *talks_helper*.

```
class TalksHelper
  attr_writer :openers, :processes

  def initialize(openers, processes)
    @openers, @processes = openers, processes
  end

  def open_everything
    @openers.each { |f| `open #{f.gsub /\s/, '\\ '}` } unless @openers.nil?
    @processes.each do |p|
      pid = fork {system p}
      Process.detach(pid)
    end unless @processes.nil?
  end
end
```

This helper class includes the code that does the actual work. This mechanism allows me to have one simple rake file per presentation and automatically launch what I need. Rake's great advantage lies in the ease with which you can interact with the underlying operating system. When you delimit strings with the backtick character (`), it automatically executes it as a shell command. The line of code that includes `open #{f.gsub /\s/, '\\ '}` really executes the *open* command from the underlying operating system (in this case, Mac OS X; you can substitute *start* in Windows), using the variable I have defined above as the argument. Using Ruby to drive the underlying operating system is much easier than writing bash scripts or batch files.

Subvert Selenium to Walk Web Pages

Selenium[‡] is an open source user acceptance testing tool for web applications. It allows you to simulate user actions by automating the browser via JavaScript. Selenium is written entirely in browser technology, so it runs in all mainstream browsers. It is an incredibly useful tool for testing web applications, regardless of the technology used to create the web application.

But I'm not here to talk about using Selenium as a testing tool. One of the ancillary projects to Selenium is a Firefox browser plug-in called Selenium IDE. Selenium IDE allows you to record your interaction with a web application as a Selenium script, which you can play back through Selenium's TestRunner or through Selenium IDE itself. While this is useful when creating tests, it is invaluable if you need to automate your interaction with a web application.

[‡] Download at *http://www.openqa.org*.

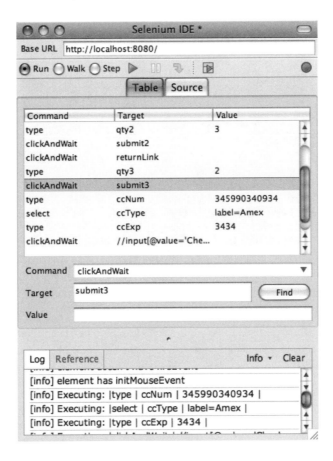

FIGURE 4-2. Selenium IDE with a script ready to run

Here is a common scenario. You are building the fourth page of a wizard-style web application. The first three pages are complete, meaning that all their interaction works correctly (including things like validations). To debug the behavior of the fourth page, you must walk through the first three pages over and over. And over. And over. You always think, "OK, this will be the last time I have to walk through these pages because I'm sure I've fixed the bug this time." But it's never the last time! This is why your test database has lots of entries for Fred Flintstone, Homer Simpson, and that ASDF guy.

Use Selenium IDE to do the walking for you. The first time you need to walk through the application to get to the fourth page, record it using Selenium IDE, which will look a lot like Figure 4-2. Now, the next time you have to walk to the fourth page, with valid values in each field, just play back the Selenium script.

Another great developer use for Selenium pops up as well. When your QA department finds a bug, they generally have some primitive way of reporting how the bug came about: a partial list of what they did, a fuzzy screen shot, or something similarly unhelpful. Have them record their bug discovery missions with Selenium IDE and report back to you. Then, you can automatically walk through the exact scenario they did, over and over, until you fix the bug. This saves both time and frustration. Selenium has essentially created an executable description of user interaction with a web application. Use it!

> NOTE
> Don't spend time doing by hand what you can automate.

Use Bash to Harvest Exception Counts

Here's an example of using bash that you might run into on a typical project. I was on a large Java project that had gone on for six years (I was just a tourist on this project, arriving in the sixth year for about eight months). One of my chores was to clean up some of the exceptions that occurred on a regular basis. The first thing I did was ask "What exceptions are being thrown and at what frequency?" Of course, no one knew, so my first task was to answer that question.

The problem was that this application excreted 2 GB logs each and every week, containing the exceptions I needed to categorize, along with a huge amount of other noise. It didn't take me long to realize that it was a waste of time to crack open this file with a text editor. So, I sat down for a little while and ended up with this:

```
#!/bin/bash

for X in $(egrep -o "[A-Z]\w*Exception" log_week.txt | sort | uniq) ;
do
    echo -n -e "processing $X\t"
    grep -c "$X" log_week.txt
done
```

Table 4-2 shows what this handy little bash script does.

TABLE 4-2. Complex bash command to harvest exception counts

Character(s)	What it's doing
egrep -o	Find all strings in the log file that have some text before "Exception", sort them, and get a distinct list
"[A-Z]\w*Exception"	The pattern that defines what an exception looks like
log_week.txt	The gargantuan log file
| sort	Pipe the results through sort, creating a sorted list of the exceptions
| uniq	Eliminate duplicate exceptions
for X in $(. . .) ;	Perform the code in the loop for each exception in the list generated above
echo -n -e "processing $X\t"	Echo to the console which exception I'm harvesting (so I can tell it's working)
grep -c "$X" log_week.txt	Find the count of this exception in the giant log file

They still use this little utility on the project. It's a good example of automating the creation of a valuable piece of project information that no one had taken the time to do before. Instead of wondering and speculating about the types of exceptions being thrown, we could look and find out exactly, making our targeted fixing of the exceptions much easier.

Replace Batch Files with Windows Power Shell

As part of the work on the Vista release of Windows, Microsoft significantly upgraded the batch language. The code name was Monad, but when it shipped it became Windows Power Shell. (For the sake of the extra trees required to spell it out every time, I'm going to keep calling it "Monad.") It is built-in to Windows Vista, but you can also use it on Windows XP by just downloading it from the Microsoft web site.

Monad borrows much of its philosophy from similar command shell languages like bash and DOS, where you can pipe the output of one command into another. The big difference is that Monad doesn't use plain text (like bash); instead, it uses objects. Monad commands (called *cmdlets*) understand a common set of objects that represent operating system constructs, like files, directories, even things like the Windows event viewer. The semantics of using it work the same as bash (the pipe operator is even the same old | symbol), but the capabilities are vast.

Here's an example. Say that you want to copy all the files that were updated since December 1, 2006 to a folder named *DestFolder*. The Monad command looks like this:

```
dir | where-object { $_.LastWriteTime -gt "12/1/2006" } |
    move-item -destination c:\DestFolder
```

Because Monad cmdlets "understand" other cmdlets and the kinds of things they output, you can write scripts much more succinctly than with other scripting languages. Here's an example. Let's say that you needed to kill all processes using more than 15 MB of memory using bash:

```
ps -el | awk '{ if ( $6 > (1024*15)) { print $3 } }'
    | grep -v PID | xargs kill
```

Pretty ugly! It uses five different bash commands, including *awk* to parse out the results of the *ps* command. Here is the equivalent Monad command:

```
get-process | where { $_.VS -gt 15M } | stop-process
```

Here, you can use the *where* command to filter the *get-process* output for a certain property (in this case, the VS property, which is the memory size).

Monad was written using .NET, which means that you also have access to standard .NET types. String manipulation, which has traditionally been tough in command shells, relies on the String methods in .NET. For example, issuing the following Monad command:

```
get-member -input "String" -membertype method
```

outputs all the methods of the String class. This is similar to using the *man* utility in *-nix.

Monad is a huge improvement over what came before in the Windows world. It offers first-class programming at the operating system–level. Many of the chores that forced developers to resort to scripting languages like Perl, Python, and Ruby can now be easily done in Monad. Because it is part of the core of the operating system, system-specific objects (like the event viewer) can be queried and manipulated.

Use Mac OS X Automator to Delete Old Downloads

Mac OS X has a graphical way of writing batch files called Automator. In many ways, it is a graphical version of Monad even though it predates Monad by several years. To create Automator workflows (Mac OS X's version of a script), drag commands from Automator's work area and "wire" together the output of one command and the input of another. Each application registers its capabilities with Automator upon installation. You can also write pieces of Automator in ObjectiveC (the underlying development language of Mac OS X) to extend it.

Here is an example Automator workflow that deletes all the old files you've downloaded if they are more than two weeks old. The workflow is shown in Figure 4-3 and consists of the following steps:

1. This workflow caches the last two weeks of downloads in a folder called *recent*.
2. Empty *recent* so that it is ready for new files.
3. Find all downloads with a modified date within the last two weeks.
4. Move them to *recent*.
5. Find all the non-folders in the *downloads* directory.
6. Delete all the files.

This workflow does more work than the Monad script above because there is no easy way in the workflow to specify that you want all the files *not* modified in the last two weeks. The best solution is to grab the ones that have been modified in the last two weeks, move them out of the way to a cache directory (named *recent*), and delete all the files in *downloads*. You would never bother to do this by hand, but because it's an automated utility, it can do extra work. One alternative would be to write a shell script in bash and incorporate it into the workflow (one of the options is to call a bash script), but then you're back to parsing out the results of a shell script to harvest the names. If you wanted to go that far, you could do the whole thing as a shell script.

Tame Command-Line Subversion

Eventually, you get to the point where you can't subvert another tool or find an open source project that does just what you want. That means it's time to build your own little jig or shim.

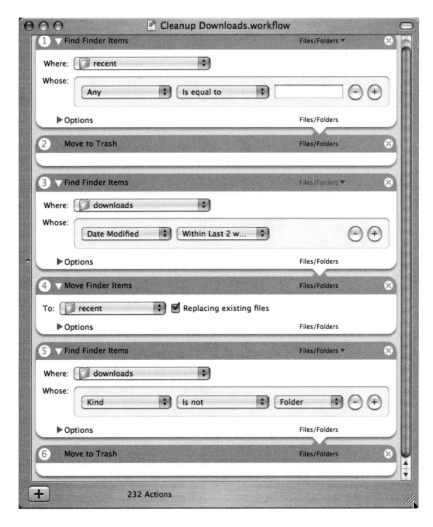

FIGURE 4-3. "Delete old downloads" workflow in Mac OS X Automator

This chapter contains lots of different ways to build tools; here are some examples of using these tools to solve problems on real projects.

I'm a big fan of the open source version control system Subversion. It is just the right combination of power, simplicity, and ease of use. Subversion is ultimately a command-line version control system, but lots of developers have created frontends for it (my favorite is the Tortoise integration with Windows Explorer). However, the real power of Subversion lies at the command line. Let's look at an example.

I tend to add files in small batches to Subversion. To use the command-line tool, you must specify each of the filenames you want to add. This isn't bad if you have only a few, but if you've added 20 files, it is cumbersome. You can use wildcards, but you'll likely grab files that are already in version control (which doesn't hurt anything, but you'll get piles of error messages that might obscure other error messages). To solve this problem, I wrote a little one-line bash command:

```
svn st | grep '^\?' | tr '^\?' ' ' |
    sed 's/[ ]*//' | sed 's/[ ]/\ /g' | xargs svn add
```

Table 4-3 shows what this one-liner does.

TABLE 4-3. Analysis of svnAddNew command sequence

Command	Result
svn st	Get Subversion status on all files in this directory and all its subdirectories. The new ones come back with a ? at the beginning and a tab before the filename.
grep '^\?'	Find all the lines that start with the ?.
tr '^\?' ' '	Replace the ? with a space (the *tr* command translates one character for another).
sed 's/[ ]*//'	Using *sed*, the stream-based editor, substitute spaces to nothing for the leading part of the line.
sed 's/[ ]/\ /g'	The filenames may have embedded spaces, so use *sed* again to substitute any remaining spaces with the escaped space character (a space with a \ in front).
xargs svn add	Take the resulting lines and pump them into the *svn add* command.

This command line took the better part of 15 minutes to implement, but I've used this little shim (or is it a jig?) hundreds of times since.

Build a SQL Splitter in Ruby

A coworker and I were working on a project where we needed to be able to parse a large (38,000-line) legacy SQL file. To make the parsing job easier, we wanted to break the monolithic file into smaller chunks of about 1,000 lines each. We thought very briefly about doing it by hand, but decided that automating it would be better. We thought about trying to do this with *sed*, but it looked like it would be complicated. We eventually settled on Ruby, and about an hour later, we had this:

```ruby
SQL_FILE = "./GeneratedTestData.sql"
OUTPUT_PATH = "./chunks of sql/"

line_num = 1
file_num = 0
Dir.mkdir(OUTPUT_PATH) unless File.exists? OUTPUT_PATH
file = File.new(OUTPUT_PATH + "chunk " + file_num.to_s + ".sql",
    File::CREAT|File::TRUNC|File::RDWR, 0644)

done, seen_1k_lines = false
IO.readlines(SQL_FILE).each do |line|
  file.puts(line)
  seen_1k_lines = (line_num % 1000 == 0) unless seen_1k_lines
  line_num += 1
  done = (line.downcase =~ /^\W*go\W*$/ or
          line.downcase =~ /^\W*end\W*$/) != nil
```

```
    if done and seen_1k_lines
      file_num += 1
      file = File.new(OUTPUT_PATH + "chunk " + file_num.to_s + ".sql",
          File::CREAT|File::TRUNC|File::RDWR, 0644)
      done, seen_1k_lines = false
    end
  end
```

This little Ruby program reads lines from the original source file until it has read 1,000 lines. Then, it starts looking for lines that have either *GO* or *END* on them. Once it finds either of those two strings, it finishes off the current file and starts another one.

We calculated that it probably would have taken us about 10 minutes to break this file up via brute force, and it took about an hour to automate it. We eventually had to do it five more times, so we almost reclaimed the time we spent automating it. But that's not the important point. Performing simple, repetitive tasks by hand makes you dumber, and it steals part of your concentration, which is your most productive asset.

> **NOTE**
> Performing simple, repetitive tasks squanders your concentration.

Figuring out a clever way to automate the task makes you smarter because you learn something along the way. One of the reasons it took us so long to complete this Ruby program was our unfamiliarity with how Ruby handled low-level file manipulation. Now we know, and we can apply that knowledge to other projects. And, we've figured out how to automate part of our project infrastructure, making it more likely that we'll find other ways to automate simple tasks.

> **NOTE**
> Finding innovative solutions to problems makes it easier to solve similar problems in the future.

Justifying Automation

When you deploy your application, it takes only three steps: run the "create tables" script on the database, copy the application files to your web server, and update the configuration files for the changes you've made to the routing for your application. Simple, easy steps. You have to do this every couple of days. So, what's the big deal? It takes only about 15 minutes.

What if your project lasts eight months? You will have to go through this ritual 64 times (actually, the pace will pick up as you near the finish line and have to deploy it a lot more often). Add it up: 64 times performing this chore × 15 minutes = 960 minutes = 16 hours = 2 work days. Two full work days to do the same thing over and over! And this doesn't take into account the number of times you accidentally forget to do one of the steps, which costs more time in debugging and repairing. If it takes you less than two days to automate the whole process, then it's a no-brainer because you get pure time savings back. But what if it takes three days to automate it—is it still worth it?

I have encountered some system administrators who write bash scripts for every task they perform. They do this for two reasons. First, if you do it once, you're almost certainly going to do it again. Bash commands are very terse by design, and it sometimes takes a few minutes even for an experienced developer to get it right. But if you ever have to do that task again, the saved commands save you time. Second, keeping all the nontrivial command-line stuff around in scripts creates living documentation of what you did, and perhaps *why* you performed some task. Saving everything you do is extreme, but storage is very cheap—much cheaper than the time it takes to recreate something. Perhaps you can compromise: don't save every single thing you do, but the second time you find yourself doing something, automate it. Chances are excellent that if you do it twice, you'll end up doing it 100 times.

Virtually everyone on *-nix systems creates aliases in their hidden *.bash_profile* configuration files, with commonly used command-line shortcuts. Here are some examples, showing the general syntax:

```
alias catout='tail -f /Users/nealford/bin/apache-tomcat-6.0.14/logs/catalina.out'
alias derby='~/bin/db-derby-10.1.3.1-bin/frameworks/embedded/bin/ij.ksh'
alias mysql='/usr/local/mysql/bin/mysql -u root'
```

Any frequently used command can appear in this file, freeing you from having to remember some incantation that does magic. In fact, this ability significantly overlaps that of using key macro tools (see "Key Macro Tools" in Chapter 2). I tend to use bash aliases for most things (less overhead with expanding the macro), but one critical category exists for which I use key macro tools. Any command line you have that contains a mixture of double and single quotes is hard to get escaped exactly right as an alias. The key macro tools handle that much better. For example, the *svnAddNew* script (shown earlier in "Tame Command-Line Subversion") started as a bash alias, but it was driving me nuts trying to get all the escaping just right. It now lives as a key macro, and life is much simpler.

> **NOTE**
> Justifying automation is about return on investment and risk mitigation.

You will see lots of chores in your projects that you would like to automate away. You have to ask yourself the following questions (and be honest with your answers):

- Will it save time in the long run?
- Is it prone to errors (because of lots of complex steps) that will rob time if done incorrectly?
- Does this task destroy my focus? (Almost any task takes you away from your locus of attention, making it harder to get back to your focused state.)
- What is the hazard of doing it wrong?

The last question is important because it addresses risk. I was once on a project with people who, for historical reasons, didn't want to create separate output directories for their code and the tests. To run the tests, we needed to create three different test suites, one for each kind of test (unit, functional, and integration). The project manager suggested that we just create the test suite by hand. But we decided to take the time to automate its creation via reflection instead. Updating the test suite by hand is error prone; it is too easy for a developer to write tests and then forget to update the test suite, meaning that his work will never get executed. We deemed the hazard of not automating as too great.

One of the things that will probably worry your project manager when you want to automate some task is that it will spiral out of control. We all have the experience of thinking that we can get something done in two hours only to have it quickly turn into four days. The best way to mitigate this risk is to *timebox* your efforts: allocate an exact amount of time for exploration and fact gathering. At the end of the timebox, re-evaluate objectively whether completely pursuing this task is feasible. Timeboxed development is about learning enough to make realistic judgments. At the end of a timebox, you may decide to use another one to find out more. I know that the clever automation task is more interesting than your project work, but be realistic. Your boss deserves real estimates.

> NOTE
> Timebox speculative development.

Don't Shave Yaks

Finally, don't allow your automation side project to turn into *yak shaving*. Yak shaving is part of the official jargon file for computer science. It describes this scenario:

1. You want to generate documentation based on your Subversion logs.
2. You try to add a Subversion hook only to discover that the Subversion library you have is incompatible and therefore won't work with your web server.
3. You start to update your web server, but realize that the version you need isn't supported by the patch level of your operating system, so you start to update your operating system.
4. The operating system upgrade has a known issue with the disk array the machine uses for backups.
5. You download an experimental patch for the disk array that should get it to work with your operating system, which works but causes a problem with the video driver.

At some point, you stop and try to remember what got you started down this road. You come to the realization that you are shaving a yak, and you stop to try to figure out what shaving a yak has to do with generating documentation for Subversion logs.

Yak shaving is dangerous because it eats up a lot of time. It also explains why estimating tasks is so often wrong: just how long *does* it take to fully shave a yak? Always keep in mind what you are trying to achieve, and pull the plug if it starts to spiral out of control.

Summary

This chapter contained lots of examples of ways to automate things, but the examples aren't really the important point. They simply serve to illustrate ways that I and others have figured out to automate common chores. Computers exist to perform simple, repetitive tasks: put them to work! Notice the repetitive stuff that you do on a daily and weekly basis and ask yourself: can I automate this away? Doing so increases the amount of time you can spend working on useful problems, instead of solving the same simple problem over and over. Performing simple tasks by hand robs some of your concentration, so eliminating those little nagging chores frees your precious mindpower for other things.

CHAPTER FIVE

Canonicality

IT'S TWO HOURS BEFORE YOUR DEMONSTRATION FOR THE BIG BOSS AND ONE OF THE critical features isn't working on your machine. This can't be. It worked just last week on Bob's machine. You go to Bob's machine and, sure enough, it works beautifully. But some of the other features that work great on your machine don't work on Bob's machine. Now it's time to panic.

Before long, the entire development team is standing around Bob's machine, trying to figure out why what he's building is different from what everyone else is building. Right before a major project milestone is the wrong (but inevitable) time for this to happen. It turns out that Bob has a newer version of a particular plug-in in his IDE and it changes the way the application runs in his environment. Of course, installing the same version of the plug-in on Bob's machine breaks other stuff. You, Bob, and all your coworkers are suffering because you're running more than one version of something important, which always gets out of sync.

A *canonical* representation refers to the simplest form without loss of information. *Canonicality* refers to the practice of eliminating duplication. In the seminal book *The Pragmatic Programmer* (Addison-Wesley), Andrew Hunt and David Thomas lay down the law: "Don't repeat yourself" (DRY). This three-word sentence has profound effects on software development. Glenn Vanderburg calls repetition "the single most diminishing force in software development." Presumably, you already agree. How do you *achieve* canonicality in software development? It's hard to even notice the problems in lots of situations, especially if non-DRYness (moistness?) is the status quo.

This chapter provides examples of how to achieve canonicality. It attacks three common sources of non-DRYness: database object-relational mapping, documentation, and communication. Each of the scenarios discussed here arose from real projects, and in each one, developers figured out ways to stay DRY.

DRY Version Control

One obvious application of canonicality has become commonplace in most development shops: version control, which qualifies as canonicality because the "real" files live in version control. Using version control has the obvious benefits of handling the versioning of your files. But it is also a great backup mechanism, keeping your source code in a safe place, away from single instances on developer machines.

I tend to prefer version control systems that don't lock files but rather merge the contents if more than one developer has made changes (called *optimistic revisions*). This is a good example of a tool that encourages good and punishes bad behavior. Checking your files into version control *early and often* encourages you to make small changes. Knowing that you'll face a merge conflict if you make long-term changes to the file encourages you to check in more often. The tool creates a useful tension, modifying the way you work in subtle but beneficial ways. Good tools are ones that encourage good behavior. Thus, I love the open source

Subversion version control system: it is very lightweight, it's free, and it does just what it is supposed to do and nothing else.

While the use of version control is virtually universal, often it is not used to its full potential. Version control can make your project artifacts as DRY as possible. Everything required to build your project should reside in version control. That includes binary files (libraries, frameworks, JAR files, build scripts, etc.). The only things that shouldn't be in version control are the configuration files particular to a developer's machine because of paths, IP addresses, etc. Even in this scenario, only the information unique to a developer's workstation should reside in a local file. Make utilities (like Ant and Nant) allow you to externalize specific information so that you can isolate just the changes.

Why keep binaries? Projects today depend on a swath of external tools and libraries. Let's say you are using one of the popular logging frameworks (like Log4J or Log4Net). If you don't build the binaries for that logging library as part of your build process, you should keep it in version control. That allows you to continue to build your software even if the framework or library in question disappears (or, more likely, introduces a breaking change in a new version). Always keep the entire universe required to build your software in version control (minus the operating system, and even that is possible with virtualization; see "Use Virtualization," later in this chapter). You can optimize retaining binaries by both keeping them in version control and on a shared network drive. That way, you don't have to deal with them on an hourly basis, but they are saved in case you need to rebuild something a year later. You never know if you will need to rebuild something. You build it until it works, then forget about it. It is panic inducing to realize you need to rebuild something from two years ago and don't have all the parts.

> **NOTE**
> Keep a *single copy* of everything you don't build in version control.

Of course, binaries add considerable bloat to your version control, which can cause problems with storage (extra space) and bandwidth (the amount of time it takes to check out the project). Two acceptable alternatives exist. Some version control packages (like Subversion) have an *externals* option, which allows you to reference one project from another. You can keep all your shared libraries in an external project referenced from several other projects. The binaries still live in version control, but they take space only once. This solves the storage problem but not the bandwidth problem.

The other solution keeps the libraries on a mapped network drive, referenced by each of the development machines. This is a scarier proposition because you have files required to build your project that no longer reside in version control. Sometimes this is the only reasonable alternative.

The unacceptable alternative is unfortunately the default in most projects: each developer has libraries on his or her own machines, sometimes in different directories. Anyone who has lived through a project setup like this knows what a nightmare maintaining this wet infrastructure can be.

YOU KNOW YOU HAVE CONFIGURATION PROBLEMS WHEN...

In a consulting company for which I worked years ago, we had a client who had an application that we had done some minor work on years before. We hadn't touched it in a long time. One of their internal developers was maintaining and enhancing it. He left to become a surfer or to otherwise "find himself," and they couldn't figure out how to get the project to build on any other machine but his. They literally tried for weeks to build the project, but the only machine on earth that would build it was this developer's laptop. In the end, they shipped us the laptop so that we could figure out what sort of magic he had done. It turned out that he was taking advantage of a little-known "feature" of Java, the *ext* directory within the runtime environment, because he was too lazy (or didn't know how) to add it to the classpath. You know you have configuration problems when you ship a laptop to a consulting company to figure out how to build your own software!

Use a Canonical Build Machine

The other process required in every development shop is continuous integration. Continuous integration is a process where you build the entire project, run tests, generate documentation, and do all the other activities that make software on a regular basis (the more often the better, generally you should build every time you check in code to version control). Continuous integration is supported by software of the same name. Ideally, the continuous integration server runs on a separate machine, monitoring your check-ins to version control. Every time you perform a code check-in, the continuous integration server springs to life, running a build command that you specify (in a build file like Ant, Nant, Rake, or Make) that usually includes performing a full build, setting up the database for testing, running the entire suite of unit tests, running code analysis, and deploying the application to perform a "smoke test." The continuous integration server redirects build responsibilities from individual machines and creates a *canonical* build location.

The canonical build machine should not include the development tool you use to create the project, only the libraries and other frameworks needed to build the application. This prevents subtle dependencies on tools from creeping into your build process. Unlike Bob and his hapless coworkers, you want to make sure that everyone builds the same thing. Having a canonical build server makes it the only "official" build for the project. Changes to development tools don't affect it.

Even single developers benefit from having a continuous integration server as the lone build machine. It prevents you from inadvertently allowing tool dependencies from creeping into your project. If you can build your application with a single command on a standalone machine, you obviously have the configuration correct.

Numerous continuous integration servers exist, both commercial and open source. CruiseControl[*] is an open source project created by ThoughtWorks, and it has ports to Java, .NET, and Ruby. Other continuous integration servers include Bamboo,[†] Hudson,[‡] TeamCity,[§] and LuntBuild.[‖]

Indirection

Platforms provide structure for heavy items. Development tools create their own platforms by providing stable ground on which you can stand to build software. But part of a platform is infrastructure, and lots of development tools create an infrastructure you can't control. Indirection allows you to take back control and become more productive.

Taming Eclipse Plug-ins

> NOTE
> Use indirection to create friendlier workspaces.

One of the best things about Eclipse is the rich ecosystem of plug-ins. One of the worst things about Eclipse is that very same rich ecosystem of plug-ins! Different team members download different versions of plug-ins. Generally, this isn't a problem, but occasionally incompatibilities exist between plug-in versions, and suddenly you have Bob's nonreproducible build. This represents a canonicality problem.

The solution is to make sure that everyone on the project has the exact same set (down to the minor version number) of all plug-ins. The larger the development team, the harder this is to manage. The creators of Eclipse anticipated this problem and allow you to configure multiple plug-in and feature locations. Inexplicably, this option resides on the Help menu, under Software Updates and Manage Configurations. Create a new configuration with the following steps:

1. Create a new subdirectory named *eclipse*. This directory should not reside within Eclipse's default directory structure.

---

[*] Download at *http://cruisecontrol.sourceforge.net/*.

[†] Download at *http://www.atlassian.com/software/bamboo/*.

[‡] Download at *https://hudson.dev.java.net/*.

[§] Download at *http://www.jetbrains.com/teamcity/*.

[‖] Download at *http://luntbuild.javaforge.com/*.

2. Create an empty placeholder file in the new directory named *.eclipseextension*. In an example of how Windows and Eclipse don't see eye-to-eye, you cannot create this file in Windows Explorer because it will not allow you to create a file with a "." as the first character. Thus, you must open a command window (either a Windows shell or bash shell will work) to create this file. The easy way to do this on operating systems that have the command is just `touch .eclipseextension`.

3. Create two (empty) directories in your new directory: *features* and *plugins*.

You must perform these steps before Eclipse will allow you to create a new configuration that points to your new directory. I'm not sure why Eclipse won't just do this for you, but it won't. At any rate, you can now use the Product Configuration dialog (which you launch from the Manage Configurations menu item). Figure 5-1 shows the Product Configuration dialog with two additional configurations defined. You can define the entire working set of plug-ins and features from there, including the JDK and all Eclipse features (the second configuration, which resides in *c:\work\eclipse*, includes the entire SDK). You can also point to just a subset of your plug-ins (as shown in the third configuration, which resides in the path *c:\work\IVE\eclipse*).

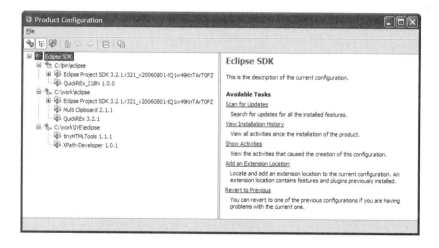

FIGURE 5-1. Product Configuration dialog in Eclipse

You may install plug-ins and features two different ways in Eclipse. You can either download the code yourself and extract the appropriate folders to the appropriate destinations. In that case, you would extract your plug-ins in the external configuration location. You can also use the Find and Install... menu item, which allows you to point to a well-defined URL and download plug-ins and features directly. In that case, Eclipse provides a button during the download process that asks in which configuration you would like to save your feature or plug-in, as shown in Figure 5-2.

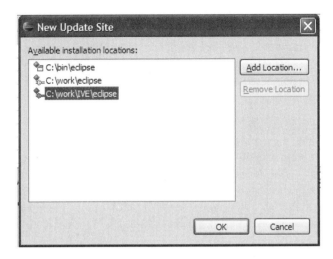

FIGURE 5-2. *Additional configured update sites*

The rest is simple: create the new product configuration in the directory that goes into version control. Set up whatever plug-ins you need for this project and do a check-in. Now, on other developer machines, check out the new configuration and point a fresh install of Eclipse to it, using the Product Configuration dialog. As changes happen on one developer's workstation, those changes will appear on other workstations the next time a version control update occurs and Eclipse is restarted.

When you create a new configuration, it lives independently of the "main" configuration. You can also selectively enable and disable configurations. This is very handy if you work on different projects, each with its own set of plug-ins. You do have to restart Eclipse when you change configurations, but that's much easier than installing and uninstalling plug-ins.

Since the time I created this solution, a canned solution called Pulse was created to manage Eclipse plug-ins.[#] This technique is still valid, of course, but someone recognized that this was such a problem that they created a tool to solve it!

Syncing JEdit Macros

I like to use JEdit as one of my general-purpose text editors. One of the nice features of JEdit is its ability to record and save macros. I work on several different machines (various Windows machines at home and a Macintosh laptop on the road). To keep my documents in sync, I have created a Subversion repository on a third machine that lives on the Internet. The repository contains my entire *Documents* directory (which is kept in My Documents on Windows and in ~/Documents on the Mac).

[#] Download at *http://www.poweredbypulse.com/*.

In JEdit, all macros are saved in the directory *[user home]\.jedit\macros,* where "[user home]" is the user's home directory on a particular machine. That means that, in my case, home on Windows is *c:\Documents and Settings\nford\,* and on the Mac it is */Users/neal/* (or, more conveniently in Unix, *~/*). The home directory isn't in the *Documents* directory. That means that the JEdit macros do not fall into the Subversion repository and therefore are not synchronized across machines.

The solution lies in indirection: make JEdit look for its macros in a location where you want them. In the *-nix operating systems (Linux, Mac OS X), you use symbolic links for this. Unfortunately, if you are on Windows 2000 or XP, you can't create symbolic links, and shortcuts won't work. The shortcut concept isn't part of the filesystem; it's a facade created by the shell. As a consequence, applications must "understand" that shortcuts actually point to something else, and JEdit wasn't written to understand shortcuts. If you are using an older version of Windows, you need some sort of symbolic link for indirection to operate (Windows Vista now has a command named *mklink* that creates real symbolic links). Fortunately, there is a free tool called Junction that handles this for you.

JUNCTION FOR WINDOWS 2000 AND XP USERS

Unix, Linux, and Mac OS X developers have links built-in to their OS. Windows users need something more than shortcuts. Junction creates duplicate entries in the table of contents for your filesystem, allowing you to create pointers to other directories. It works at the operating system–level, so all applications (including Windows itself) respect the pointer that it creates.

junction is a command-line tool that allows you to create and delete hard links. For example, if you wanted to create a link called "myproject" in the current directory that points to another (deeply nested) directory, you would issue the following command:

```
junction myproject \My Documents\Projects\Sisyphus\NextGen
```

The pseudofolder *myproject* acts as an operating system–level pointer to your *\My Documents \Projects\Sisyphus\NextGen* folder.

Now that we have real indirection on all operating systems, I can create a directory within *Documents* that holds all my JEdit macros. On Windows, I use a junction link to create a pointer called "macros" from the directory *c:\Documents and Settings\nford\.jedit.* Similarly, on OS X, I create a symbolic link named "macros" in the *~/.jedit* directory. Both the junction and symbolic link point to the directory that resides within the *Documents* directory (and therefore within the Subversion repository). Figure 5-3 illustrates this solution.

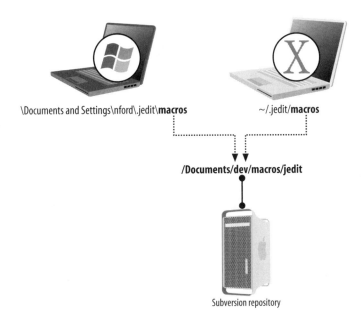

\Documents and Settings\nford\.jedit**macros**   ~/.jedit/**macros**

/**Documents/dev/macros/jedit**

Subversion repository

FIGURE 5-3. JEdit macro locations on different operating systems

Now, I blissfully record macros on either machine and perform a Subversion check-in for all my work. When I do a checkout on the other machine, all the macros come down into the *Documents* folder and, because I have "fooled" JEdit into looking into that folder instead of its default location, all the macros I have recorded appear right away.

> **NOTE**
> Use indirection to keep your life in sync.

Using indirection for canonicality can be nested multiple levels deep. At one point, I worked on multiple projects, each one with customized macros. I wanted to share the macros using the indirection principle, but the other teams were only interested in the macros that pertained to their projects. Spamming them with all the macros from JEdit's macros folder via indirection would violate the *focus* productivity principle, which seeks to eliminate noise.

Because JEdit supports directories in its macros folder, the solution was simple: create links or junctions for individual projects in their own directories and place those specialized directories in each version control repository. The directory that JEdit looks at for its macros is still a link (or junction), and it contains other links/junctions to other external directories in version control.

You can layer indirection in as many layers as you would like by having one indirection link point to another indirection link, creating a chain of indirection. The main limiting factor is the tool you are using: if it relies on individual files for shared resources and you are on Windows, you can't use this technique. However, that should be a fairly short list of tools, and if you find yourself having to use an overly restrictive tool, maybe it is time to find another.

TextMate Bundles

TextMate[*] is a sophisticated programmer's editor for Mac OS X. One of the features that makes it so powerful is the concept of a *code snippet* (known in other tools as a live template). It is also ported to Windows in the form of the E Text Editor.[†]

The snippets in TextMate are kept within a *bundle*, which is a collection of files in Mac OS X in the package format. Mac OS X uses this concept to provide installers for applications that consist of a large number of files. Applications like TextMate can also use the Mac OS X package concept for its bundles.

One of the nice features in TextMate is the ability to share these bundles by finding them in the filesystem and dragging them to another location, presumably on a shared network drive. The bundles are stored in *~/Library/Application Support/TextMate/Bundles*. Once you have extracted a bundle this way, you can double-click on the bundle to install it on another machine. In other words, TextMate has thought about sharing its bundles and has put them in a format that allows them to self-install on another machine. Hats off to the creators of TextMate for embracing the ideals of *The Productive Programmer*!

But the ability to share by copy and paste is less than optimal. What happens when you add new snippets to your bundle? The other copies of that bundle obviously won't be able to take advantage of those changes. Reuse by copy and paste is evil, even if you are copying configurations from one machine to another.

> NOTE
> No matter what you are copying and pasting, resuse by copy and paste is evil.

Even though the bundles look like single files in OS X's Finder, they are actually folders, which means that you can represent them via links. Just as in the previous JEdit example, you can create a link in the *Bundles* folder at *~/Library/Application Support/TextMate/Bundles* that points to a "real" folder that lives in version control. This allows everyone on the development team access to the same set of bundles, so when someone creates an incredibly useful snippet, the entire team can take advantage of it upon the next update cycle from version control.

[*] Download at *http://macromates.com/*.

[†] Download at *http://www.e-texteditor.com/*.

Canonical Configuration

Getting machines set up all the same way is one of the perpetual headaches on projects. Some projects resort to mirroring entire machines down to the operating system-level (which is the only way for some development environments; see the next section "Use Virtualization"). Using indirection, you can ease this problem significantly.

For example, Emacs keeps all of its configuration information in a file named *.emacs*, which lives in the user's home directory. (It keeps some stuff like history in a directory named *.emacs.d*.) What if you want to share that configuration across machines? You can use indirection and a symbolic link (on *-nix machines) to keep the "real" *.emacs* in version control and let Emacs point to the link. Unfortunately, you cannot do this with Junction in Windows 2000 or XP, but you can with symbolic links in Windows Vista.

Another common pain point in projects revolves around the code snippets developers use to accelerate coding. I discussed how to do this in TextMate earlier, but that doesn't help much if you aren't using TextMate, does it? You can create code snippets in popular IDEs. Unfortunately, there is no standard way to do this, so I'll cover how to do it in a couple of popular Java IDEs: IntelliJ and Eclipse.

Sharing snippets (called live templates in IntelliJ) is quite easy because they are kept in a directory (for example, on Mac OS X they live in */Users/nealford/Library/Preferences/ IntelliJIDEA70/templates*) and each snippet has its own file. Thus, to share IntelliJ snippets, just move a canonical version of the snippets directory to version control and create a symbolic link (or junction link) from the original location to the new home in version control.

Unfortunately, it's much harder to do this in Eclipse because Eclipse keeps snippets buried in a Java properties file. The custom snippets are the values of one of the properties, encoded in XML as the property value. No, I'm not kidding. It's almost like they are making it as hard as possible to get to them programatically! A small section of this file looks like this (with wrapping added):

```
#Tue Feb 12 09:45:01 EST 2008
org.eclipse.jdt.ui.overrideannotation=true
spelling_locale_initialized=true
org.eclipse.jdt.ui.javadoclocations.migrated=true
proposalOrderMigrated=true
org.eclipse.jdt.ui.formatterprofiles.version=11
useQuickDiffPrefPage=true
org.eclipse.jdt.ui.text.custom_templates=<?xml version\="1.0"
  encoding\="UTF-8"?><templates><template autoinsert\="true" context\="java"
  deleted\="false" description\="" enabled\="true" name\="my_test">
  @Test public void ${var}() {\n\n}</template></templates>
org.eclipse.jdt.ui.text.code_templates_migrated=true
```

Eclipse does provide a way to import and export snippets via the Preferences dialog. Import and export essentially copy and paste, but that's the easiest way to share the snippets. The other complication is that add-on editors may keep their snippets in different locations: there is no standard place in Eclipse for snippets. Because Eclipse keeps its snippets in text files, you could create a script that saves and regenerates the properties file on a regular basis, but that is a lot of work.

Use Virtualization

NOTE
Use virtualization to canonicalize dependencies for your projects.

Several years ago, I used the indirection aspect of canonicality to streamline development in .NET while trying to recreate a Visual Studio environment that we'd used on another project. There's a rich ecosystem of third-party components for Visual Studio. The catch is that using third-party components means that every application development environment is subtly different.

Client A uses this widget, but you have to make sure not to use it for Client B because they don't own a license for it. Once you install components on the developer's machine, they become part of the operating system. Some client setups could take a week just to get the environment tweaked to do work. The problem is one of isolation: you can't encapsulate the development environment (or the developed application) at any level lower than the operating system.

We built our applications using virtual instances of the operating system. The premier tool for doing this at the time was VMWare, and it had just gotten Really Good. We realized that we could take a generic Windows ghost and install all the necessary developer tools on a VMWare image and develop on it. The speed hit at the time wasn't terrible, and it allowed us clean-room development for each client. When that phase of the project concluded, we saved the VMWare image out to a server.

Two years later, when that client came back for enhancements, we started up that application's development environment just like the day we left it. This approach saved us days of downtime, and made developing for multiple clients a breeze. Client A needs some minor tweaks while I'm working on Client B's application. No problem—just bounce between virtual machine images. This approach offers other tangible benefits as well. Building a development environment from a clean install of the operating system and developer tools flushes out hidden dependencies between the operating system, tools, office suites, etc.

DRY Impedance Mismatches

Have you ever experienced a telephone conversation with an annoying echo? That's an *impedance mismatch*, caused when the signals aren't perfectly synchronized. Impedance mismatch is a term from electrical engineering that has leaked over into the software world because it describes some of our problems.

In software, impedance mismatch is one of the common causes of DRY violations. An impedance mismatch occurs at the boundary of two abstraction styles: set-based to object-based, or procedural to object orientation. Because you try to reconcile the two abstraction styles, you end up with repetition around the boundaries.

Data Mapping

NOTE
Don't let object-relational mapping tools (O/R mappers) violate canonicality.

One of the constant headaches we face on projects that deal with data is the impedance mismatch between relational databases and object-oriented programming languages. Solving this mismatch has gradually led us to O/R mappers like Hibernate, nHibernate, iBatis, and others. Using an O/R mapper introduces repetition in projects where we have essentially the same information in three places: in the database schema, in an XML mapping document, and in a class file. This represents two violations of the DRY principle.

The solution to this problem is to create a single representation and generate the other two. The first step is deciding who is the "official" holder of this knowledge. For example, if the database is the canonical source, generate the XML mapping and the corresponding class files.

In this example, I used Groovy (the scripting language dialect of Java) to solve the mismatch. On the project that spawned this example, the developers had no control over the database schema. Thus, I decided that the database is the canonical representation of the data. I was using the open source iBatis[‡] SQL mapping tool (which doesn't generate SQL; it merely handles mapping classes to SQL results).

The first step entailed harvesting the schema information from the database:

```
class GenerateEventSqlMap {
    static final SQL =
        ["sqlUrl":"jdbc:derby:/Users/jNf/work/derby_data/schedule",
            "driverClass":"org.apache.derby.jdbc.EmbeddedDriver"]
    def _file_name
    def types = [:]

    def GenerateEventSqlMap(file_name) {
        _file_name = file_name
    }

    def columnNames() {❶
        Class.forName(SQL["driverClass"])
        def rs = DriverManager.getConnection(SQL["sqlUrl"]).createStatement().
            executeQuery("select * from event where 1=0")

        def rsmd = rs.getMetaData()
        def columns = []
        for (index in 1..rsmd.getColumnCount()) {
```

[‡] Download at *http://ibatis.apache.org/*.

```
            columns << rsmd.getColumnName(index)
            types.put(camelize(rsmd.getColumnName(index)),
        rsmd.getColumnTypeName(index))
        }
        return columns
    }

    def camelized_columns() {❷
        def cc = []
        columnNames().each { c ->
            cc << camelize(c)
        }
        cc
    }

    def camelize(name) {
        def newName = name.toLowerCase().split("_").collect() {
            it.substring(0, 1).toUpperCase() + it.substring(1, it.length())
        }.join()
        newName.substring(0, 1).toLowerCase() +
      newName.substring(1, newName.length())
    }

    def columnMap() {
        def columnMap = [:]
        for (colName in columnNames())
            columnMap.put(camelize(colName), colName)
        return columnMap
    }

    def create_mapping_file() {❸
        def writer = new StringWriter()
        def xml = new MarkupBuilder(writer)
        xml.sqlMap(namespace:'event') {
            typeAlias(alias:'Event',
        type:'com.nealford.conf.canonicality.Event')
            resultMap(id:'eventResult', class:'Event') {
                columnMap().each() {key, value ->❹
          result(property:"${key}", column:"${value}")
                }}
            select(id:'getEvents', resultMap:'eventResult',
                    'select * from event where id = ?')
            select(id:"getEvent",
        resultClass:"com.nealford.conf.canonicality.Event",
                    "select * from event where id = #value#")
        }

        new File(_file_name).withWriter { w ->
            w.writeLine("${writer.toString()}")
        }
    }
}
```

❶ The columnNames method uses low-level Java Database Connectivity (JDBC) to harvest the column names from the database.

❷ The camelized_columns returns the database column names changed into typical Java method names.

❸ The create_mapping_file uses a Groovy builder to make it easy to output an XML document.

❹ One of the benefits of using a builder is terser syntax compared to creating an XML document using something like DOM. You can also take advantage of loops (here via the each method) to generate XML from code.

Outside the `BuildEventSqlMap` class, I invoked the class by constructing it and tell it to generate the XML mapping file:

```
def generator = new GenerateEventSqlMap("/Users/jNf/temp/EventSqlMap.xml")
generator.create_mapping_file()
```

The end result of this invocation is the mapping file, suitable for consumption by iBatis:

```
<sqlMap namespace='event'>
    <typeAlias type='com.nealford.conf.canonicality.Event' alias='Event' />
    <resultMap id='eventResult' class='Event'>
      <result property='description' column='DESCRIPTION' />
      <result property='eventKey' column='EVENT_KEY' />
      <result property='start' column='START' />
      <result property='eventType' column='EVENT_TYPE' />
      <result property='duration' column='DURATION' />
    </resultMap>
    <select resultMap='eventResult' id='getEvents'>
      select * from event where id = ?
    </select>
    <select resultClass='com.nealford.conf.canonicality.Event' id='getEvent'>
      select * from event where id = #value#
    </select>
</sqlMap>
```

Generating the XML SQL map solves one of our repetition problems (I now generate the mapping file directly from the database schema as part of the build process). I used the same technique to generate the class file. In fact, I can leverage the same infrastructure because I've already harvested the column names from the database. To generate the class file, I built a `ClassBuilder` class:

```
class ClassBuilder {
    def imports = []
    def fields = [:]
    def file_name
    def package_name

    def ClassBuilder(imports, fields, file_name, package_name) {
        this.imports = imports
        this.fields = fields
        this.file_name = file_name
        this.package_name = package_name
    }

    def write_imports(w) {
        imports.each { i ->
            w.writeLine("import ${i};")
        }
        w.writeLine("")
    }

    def write_classname(w) {
        def class_name_with_extension = file_name.substring(
      file_name.lastIndexOf("/") + 1, file_name.length());
```

```
            w.writeLine("public class " +
                class_name_with_extension.substring(0,
            class_name_with_extension.length() - 5) + " {")
    }

    def write_fields(w) {
        fields.each { name, type ->
            w.writeLine("\t${type} ${name};");
        }
        w.writeLine("")
    }

    def write_properties(w) {❶
        fields.each { name, type ->
            def cap_name = name.charAt(0).toString().toUpperCase() +
        name.substring(1)
            w.writeLine("\tpublic ${type} get${cap_name}() {")
            w.writeLine("\t\treturn ${name};\n\t}\n");

            w.writeLine("\tpublic void set${cap_name}(${type} ${name}) {")
            w.writeLine("\t\tthis.${name} = ${name};\n\t}\n")
        }
    }

    def generate_class_file() {❷
        new File(file_name).withWriter { w ->
            w.writeLine("package ${package_name};\n")
            write_imports(w)
            write_classname(w)
            write_fields(w)
            write_properties(w)
            w.writeLine("}")
        }
    }
}
```

❶ Groovy's flexible string syntax (like Ruby, it allows you to reference member variables in strings using substitutions) makes it easy to generate standard Java constructs like get/set methods.

❷ This method uses all the helpers to write out a standard Java class file.

In the script, after I called the methods to generate the XML mapping file, I called the ClassBuilder to build the corresponding class from the same information:

```
TYPE_MAPPING = ["INTEGER" : "int", "VARCHAR" : "String"]
def fields = [:]
generator.camelized_columns().each { name ->
    fields.put(name, TYPE_MAPPING[generator.types[name]]);
}
new ClassBuilder(["java.util.Date"], fields,
    "/Users/jNf/temp/Event.java", "com.nealford.conf.canonicality").
  generate_class_file()
```

The result of this invocation yields the Java class file:

```
package com.nealford.conf.canonicality;

import java.util.Date;

public class Event {
```

```
      String description;
      int eventKey;
      String start;
      int eventType;
      int duration;

      public String getDescription() {
        return description;
      }

      public void setDescription(String description) {
        this.description = description;
      }

      public int getEventKey() {
        return eventKey;
      }

      public void setEventKey(int eventKey) {
        this.eventKey = eventKey;
      }

      public String getStart() {
        return start;
      }

      public void setStart(String start) {
        this.start = start;
      }

      public int getEventType() {
        return eventType;
      }

      public void setEventType(int eventType) {
        this.eventType = eventType;
      }

      public int getDuration() {
        return duration;
      }

      public void setDuration(int duration) {
        this.duration = duration;
      }

    }
```

Of course, this is just a DAO (data access object) with no behavior: it is merely a collection of get/set methods. If you need to add behavior to this entity, you can subclass the DAO to add methods. Never hand-edit a generated file because it will be regenerated the next time you perform a build.

NOTE
Add behavior to generated code via extension, open classes, or partial classes.

To add behavior to your generated code, you can inherit (in languages like Java), use open classes (in languages like Ruby, Groovy, and Python), or use partial classes (in languages like C#).

Now, I've solved all the DRY problems in my O/R mapping code. The Groovy script runs as part of the build process so that any time the database schema changes, it automatically generates the corresponding mapping file and the Java class to which it maps.

Migrations

Another situation where duplication creeps into projects also arises from the impedance mismatch between code and SQL. Lots of projects treat source code and SQL as completely separate artifacts, sometimes created by entirely separate groups of developers. Yet, for the source code to function correctly, it must rely on a certain version of the database schema and data. There are a couple of ways to solve this problem, one framework is specific and the other was designed to work across frameworks and languages.

> NOTE
> Always keep code and schemas in sync.

Rake migrations

One of the many cool things about the Ruby on Rails web development framework is the idea of *migrations.* A migration is a Ruby source file that handles versioning your database schemas, helping keep them in sync with your source code. Presumably, you'll make database changes (both in schema and test data) at the same time you make code changes. Managing your database via migrations allows you to check both changes into version control at the same time, enabling your version control to act as the keeper of snapshots of code + data.

A Rails migration is generated by one of the software factories that comes with Rails, which is essentially a Ruby script that creates a source file with two methods: up (where you place your changes to the database) and down (where you write the symmetrical operation, the "undo" for whatever you did in up). Each migration is named with a numeric prefix (for example, *001_create_user_table.rb*). Rails comes with Rake tasks to play the migrations in forward order to make changes and backward order to undo those changes.

Here is an example Rails migration that creates a table with a few columns:

```
class CreateProducts < ActiveRecord::Migration
  def self.up
    create_table :products do |t|
      t.column :title, :string
      t.column :description, :text
      t.column :image_url, :string
    end
  end

  def self.down
```

```
      drop_table :products
    end
  end
```

In this migration, I created a `Product` table with three columns in the up method, and dropped it in the down one.

Migrations allow you to stay DRY by keeping the schema information in code rather than in a database. One of the side benefits of this design is the Rails support for multiple deployment targets. In the Rails configuration file *database.yml*, you define environments (for example, "development," "test," and "production"). Migrations allow you to put any one of the development environment databases in a particular state simply by running the migrations against that environment.

The only downside to migration is that it is tightly tied to the Rails framework, which is great if you are using Rails but doesn't help you in other frameworks.

dbDeploy

However, all is not lost if you aren't using Rails. dbDeploy is an open source framework that provides some of the benefits of migrations in a platform-agnostic way. Written in Java, it supports a wide (and growing) list of database servers, including all the mainstream ones.

dbDeploy works by creating a baseline SQL snapshot of the database (including DDL and data). As developers make changes to the data, they create change scripts as sequentially numbered files that embody the changes. dbDeploy helps manage generating actual SQL scripts to run against your database. It keeps track of the changes in a database (named `dbdeploy`) and table (named `changelog` by default) that you add to your database. dbDeploy comes with scripts for supported databases to create the `changelog` table for you. The script to create it for MS-SQL server looks like this:

```
USE dbdeploy
  GO

  CREATE TABLE changelog (
    change_number INTEGER NOT NULL,
    delta_set VARCHAR(10) NOT NULL,
    start_dt DATETIME NOT NULL,
    complete_dt DATETIME NULL,
    applied_by VARCHAR(100) NOT NULL,
    description VARCHAR(500) NOT NULL
  )
  GO

  ALTER TABLE changelog ADD CONSTRAINT Pkchangelog PRIMARY KEY (change_number, delta_set)
  GO
```

NOTE
Use migrations to create repeatable snapshots of schema changes.

Although not as comprehensive as migrations, dbDeploy still solves part of the problem of having schema and code live in two completely separate places. Allowing you to manage the changes to your database programmatically gives you a better chance of keeping the two in sync and avoiding the inevitable impedance mismatches between code and data definitions.

DRY Documentation

> **NOTE**
> Out-of-date documentation is worse than none because it is actively misleading.

Documentation is a classic battleground between management and developers: managers want more and developers want to create less. It is also a battleground in the war against noncanonical representations. Developers should be able to make changes to code aggressively, to improve its structure and allow it to evolve. If you must have documentation for all your code, it must evolve at the same time. But most of the time, they get out of sync because of schedule pressure, lack of motivation (because, let's face it, writing code is more fun than writing documentation), and other factors.

> **NOTE**
> For managers, documentation is about risk mitigation.

Out-of-date documentation creates the risk of spreading misinformation (which is ironic, given that part of its purpose is to reduce risk). The best way to prevent documentation from getting out-of-date is to generate as much of it as possible. This section covers a couple of scenarios that make that possible.

SVN2Wiki

On one of my projects, we had a problem passing information around. Developers were scattered around the world in Bangalore, New York, and Chicago. We were sharing a single source control repository (in Chicago) and keeping track of important decisions on a wiki (we were using the open source Instiki). At the end of every day, each developer was responsible for updating the wiki to indicate what he or she had done that day. You can guess how well that worked considering the inevitable mad rush to leave the office and catch trains that occurred at the end of the day. We tried nagging the developers, which only irritated everyone.

Then we realized that we were actually violating the canonicality principle because we were asking the developers to document stuff they had already documented—in their comments when posting to version control. All the developers were good about writing descriptive comments. We decided to leverage that existing resource, and to that end, we created SVN2Wiki, a little utility designed as a Subversion plug-in. When Subversion performs

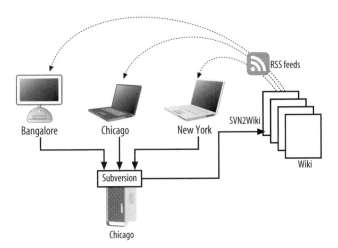

FIGURE 5-4. *SVN2Wiki setup bridges geographic boundaries*

operations, you can write programs that it will run for you. SVN2Wiki sits and waits for Subversion to call it when someone checks in code. It then harvests the comments added by that developer pair and posts them to the wiki.

After posting the comments automatically, we realized that our wiki supported RSS feeds. That meant that all the developers (and, it turned out, the manager) could subscribe to the wiki feeds to find out what had happened in the code base since the last time they looked. This whole setup is diagrammed in Figure 5-4.

The code for SVN2Wiki is simplicity itself. We wrote it in C# (it should be easy to port to other languages). In fact, the most complex code in SVN2Wiki concerned getting the entries to post on dated pages:

```
namespace Tools.SVN2Wiki {
    public class SVN2Wiki {
        private const CONFIG =
            "c:/repository/hooks/svn2wiki-config.xml";
        private SubversionViewer subversionViewer;
        private string revision;
        private string repository;
        private SVN2WikiConfiguration config;
        private Wiki wiki;

        private static void Main(string[] args) {
          string repository = args[0];
          string revision = args[1];

          //get configuration
          SVN2WikiConfiguration config =
              new SVN2WikiConfiguration(CONFIG);
          config.loadConfiguration();

          Wiki wiki = new WikiUpdates(new HttpInvokerImpl(),
              config.WikiURL);
```

```
        SVN2Wiki svn2wiki = new SVN2Wiki(new SubversionViewerImpl(),
            revision, repository, config, wiki);
        svn2wiki.processUpdate();
    }

    public SVN2Wiki(SubversionViewer subversionViewer,
                    string revision,
                    string repository,
                    SVN2WikiConfiguration config,
                    Wiki wiki) {
        this.subversionViewer = subversionViewer;
        this.repository = repository;
        this.revision = revision;
        this.config = config;
        this.wiki = wiki;
    }

    public SVNCommit getCommitData() {
        string machine = subversionViewer.svnLook(
            "author -r " + revision + " " + repository);
        string date = subversionViewer.svnLook(
            "date -r " + revision + " " + repository);
        string comments = subversionViewer.svnLook(
            "log -r " + revision + " " + repository);
        string[] dateToParse = date.Split(' ');
        date = dateToParse[0] + " " + dateToParse[1] + " " + dateToParse[2];
        return new SVNCommit(machine, DateTime.Parse(date), comments);
    }

    public void processUpdate() {
        SVNCommit commit = getCommitData();

        //for each updater in the config file
        foreach (UpdaterConfiguration updater in config.Updaters) {
            if (needToPostSVNCommit(commit, updater)) {
                Console.WriteLine("Posting to " + updater.MenuPage);
                wiki.UpdatesListPage = updater.MenuPage;
                wiki.UpdatesPageNamePrefix = updater.UpdatePagePrefix;
                Console.WriteLine("posting commit:");
                Console.WriteLine(commit.Machine + " " +
                    commit.CommittedOn);
                wiki.postUpdate(commit);
            }
        }
    }

    public bool needToPostSVNCommit(SVNCommit commit,
                                    UpdaterConfiguration updater) {
        string[] users = updater.ExcludeUsers.Split(',');
        if (arrayContainsString(users, commit.Machine))
            return false;
        if (updater.ExcludePaths.Length == 0)
            return true;
        else
        {
            string[] paths = updater.ExcludePaths.Split(',');
            string[] changedDirectories =
                getChangedDirectories(repository, revision);
            foreach (string changedDir in changedDirectories) {
                bool changedDirInExcludePaths = false;
                foreach (string path in paths) {
                    Console.WriteLine("Path = " + path);
```

```
        if (changedDir.StartsWith(path))
            changedDirInExcludePaths = true;
      }

      if (!changedDirInExcludePaths)
          return true;
    }
  }

  return false;
}

private bool arrayContainsString(string[] array, string toFind) {
  foreach (string a in array)
    if (a == toFind) return true;
 return false;
}

private string[] getChangedDirectories(string repository,
                                       string revision) {
  return subversionViewer.svnLook(
      "dirs-changed -r " + revision + " " + repository).Split('\n');
    }
  }
}
```

SVN2Wiki is a great example of *living documentation*. Most documentation for projects is lame because it no longer has relevance. Because we were so geographically dispersed, using the wiki turned out to be the best thing for our project in terms of documenting all the decisions and (with SVN2Wiki) even our code check-ins. We put all the important information about the project there: meeting agendas with summaries of decisions, informal diagrams we drew on whiteboards and then captured with digital cameras, etc. Wikis allow searching (the one we used allowed regular expression searches, so we could revisit decisions any time). At the end of the project, we exported the entire wiki as HTML, and we had documentation so good that you could almost recreate the project from it. When you think about it, that's the goal of documenting your work in the first place: to create a reliable source of what you did and why.

NOTE
Always keep "living" documentation.

Class Diagrams

NOTE
Anything that takes real effort to create makes its creator irrationally attached to it.

Even though agile development tries to be as informal as possible, you still sometimes need diagrams to illustrate the relationships between classes or other artifacts. You may be tempted to use an elaborate tool to draw your diagrams, but you should resist that temptation. If it takes any effort at all to create something, that means that it will take effort to change it. Your irrational attachment to a diagram is proportional to the effort it took to create it. If it took you 15 minutes, you'll subconsciously try to avoid changes because in the back of your mind you're thinking of how long it took to create it.

> NOTE
> Whiteboard + digital camera trumps a CASE tool.

Therefore, low-ritual artifacts are best, and my favorite is the lowly drawing on a whiteboard. It takes virtually no effort (so you don't mind changing it). It's easy to draw collaboratively (which most of the tools won't allow). When you're done, snap a picture of it with a digital camera and make it part of your documentation. You really need it only until you embody it in code, and then the code can speak for itself.

> NOTE
> Generate all the technical documents you can.

To allow the code to speak for itself, you should get a tool that produces diagrams from your code. A good example of one such tool is yDoc, a commercial diagramming tool, which produces UML diagrams with hyperlinked relationships directly from code. An example UML diagram from a project is shown in Figure 5-5. Some IDEs (such as Visual Studio) will offer to generate diagrams for you, but they are sometimes hard to automate. Ideally, you should generate diagrams at the same time you compile your code (using something like a continuous integration server). That way, you never have to think, "Are my diagrams up-to-date?" because they always live in an up-to-date state.

> NOTE
> Never keep two copies of the same thing (like code and a diagram describing it).

If you are going to draw your diagrams first, use the tool to generate the code. If you create informal diagrams using the whiteboard approach and need more formal diagrams later, generate them from code. Otherwise, they will always get out of sync.

Database Schemas

Just like class diagrams, database schemas are a dangerous area for needless repetition. SchemaSpy[§] is an open source tool that does for database entity/relationship diagrams what yDoc does for code. It attaches to the database and produces table information (including metadata) and relationship diagrams like the one shown in Figure 5-6.

[§] Download at *http://schemaspy.sourceforge.net/*.

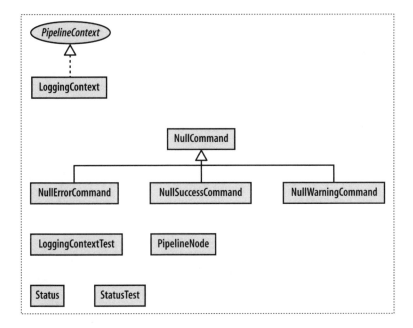

FIGURE 5-5. UML diagram generated by yDoc

Summary

NOTE
Repetition is the single most diminishing force in software development.

Repetition creeps up on projects in sneaky ways. It sometimes takes ingenuity to figure out ways around it. Glenn Vanderburg, a wise seer of software development, sums it up nicely:

Duplication is evil. Evil, I say!

Getting really maniacal about DRY has several positive effects:

- You get good at refactoring.
- You end up with a pretty decent design—usually not the best, but much better than what teams usually come up with.
- You end up rediscovering some of the more common patterns, so you actually understand them.
- The experienced people on the team have plenty of opportunities to teach about various encapsulation mechanisms, design tactics, etc., because the junior people often can't

figure out how to eliminate duplication and have to ask for help. (And when you explain these things in context, they tend to stick a little better.)

Once a programmer gets more experienced, he will start noticing the times when maybe the rules should be relaxed a little, because if you're too rigorous about duplication, sometimes you pay readability or performance penalties. But that doesn't change the fact that DRY really is the fundamental principle of good code.

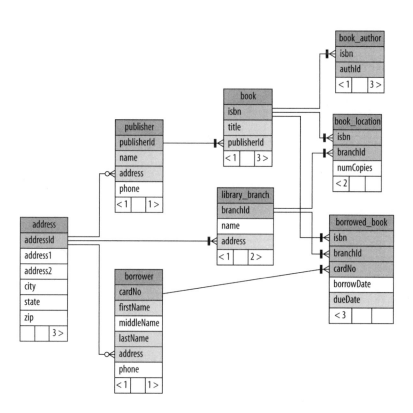

FIGURE 5-6. Relationship diagram produced by SchemaSpy

PART II

Practice

The chapters in Part II, *Practice*, offer numerous suggestions for ways to improve your code. The advice here mostly cuts across languages, abstractions, and development methodologies. Chances are very good that you already apply some or most of these practices. But, even if you fastidiously manage the life cycle of your objects (good citizenship), you might still see a new solution here. Feel free to skim or even skip chapters if you think you already have something covered. But, fair warning: I occasionally throw in some surprises, just to keep you on your toes.

CHAPTER SIX

Test-Driven Design

UNIT TESTING IS WELL ESTABLISHED AS A BENEFICIAL CODE-HYGIENE PRACTICE. Tested code provides greater confidence that the intent matches the result. Test-driven development (TDD) goes even further, insisting that you write tests before you write the code. When comparing software "engineering" to other engineering disciplines (which always requires a good handful of tortured metaphors), major differences pop up. We don't have centuries of mathematics to rely upon in software. The science of software development hasn't been around long enough (and we may never get to that level of sophistication). We also can't take advantage of the economy of scale in traditional engineering. For example, the Golden Gate Bridge contains more than 1,000,000 rivets. You can bet that the engineers who designed that bridge knew the stress characteristics of those rivets and used that number multiplied by 1,000,000 to tell them important things about the stress on the bridge. A piece of software may also have 1,000,000 pieces, but they are all different. We can't take advantage of the scale and multiplicity that "regular" engineers can. But developers do have an advantage: we can manufacture our components very easily and write code that verifies our components do what we intended them to do. Because it is vanishingly cheap to write software to test software, we can apply our own version of verification through levels of testing: unit testing, functional testing, integration testing, and user acceptance.

> NOTE
> Testing *is* the engineering rigor of software development.

Rigorously applied TDD has other design benefits as well, so many that I usually refer to TDD as test-driven *design*. TDD forces you to think about code in a different way. Instead of just writing a pile of code and then writing the tests for it, TDD forces you to think through the testing process before you write the code. TDD creates *consumption awareness*: when you create a unit test, you are creating the first consumer of the code under development. This forces you to think about how the rest of the world will use this class. Every developer has the experience of writing a class in one big bunch, making assumptions along the way. Then, when it comes time to actually use the class, you realize that some of your assumptions were wrong, and you have to refactor the original code. TDD requires that you create the first consumer before you write the code, making you think about how other code will eventually use the code under development.

TDD also forces you to mock out dependent objects. For example, if you develop a `Customer` class with an `addOrder` method, you must collaborate with an `Order` object. If you create the dependent object within the `addOrder` method, it requires that the `Order` object exist before you can test the `Customer` class. Mock objects allow you to create a "fake" version of the dependent class for testing purposes. You must think about the interaction between the two objects at exactly the right time: as you are developing the first of the two classes.

TDD encourages you to pass dependent objects via fields or parameters, leaving the construction of the dependent objects elsewhere (because you can't mock out a dependency if the method fires the constructor itself). This tends to move object construction to well-defined boundary layers, making it easier to track allocation and referencing (so that you don't inadvertently hold accidental references to objects, preventing them from garbage collection because they never go out of scope). TDD also virtually forces you to have very small, cohesive methods because you must write tests that test only one thing. Your methods tend to do only one thing as well, making them adhere more closely to the SLAP principle (covered in Chapter 13).

Evolving Tests

Let's look at an example of the design benefits that TDD affords. To demonstrate them, we need a problem that isn't so trivial as to be a throwaway, but not so complex that we get caught up in the details. A perfect candidate (pun intended) is a *perfect number* finder. A perfect number is a number whose factors (minus the number itself) add up to the number. For example, 6 is a perfect number because the factors of 6 (1, 2, 3, and 6) minus the 6 add up to 6. Let's write some code in Java to find perfect numbers.

TDDing Unit Tests

The following code was written without TDD, just by applying simple logic and some minor mathematical optimizations:

```java
public class PerfectNumberFinder {

    public static boolean isPerfect(int number) {
        // get factors
        List<Integer> factors = new ArrayList<Integer>();
        factors.add(1);
        factors.add(number);
        for (int i = 2; i < Math.sqrt(number) + 1; i++)❶
            if (number % i == 0) {
                factors.add(i);
                if ( number / i != i )❷
                    factors.add(number / i);
            }

        // sum the factors
        int sum = 0;
        for (Integer i : factors)
            sum += i;

        // decide if its perfect
        return sum - number == number;
    }
}
```

❶ If you can harvest the numbers in pairs, you only have to go up to the square root of the number. For example, for the number 28, when you find the factor 2, you can also harvest the number 14, the symmetrical factor.

❷ The code `number / i != i` is present to make sure that you don't add the same number to the list twice. Because you're harvesting symmetrical pairs, what happens when the factor is the same? For example, in the case of 16, when you get the factor 4, you'll need to add it to the list only once.

This code has a single static method that returns true or false depending on the perfection of the passed number. The first step gets the factors. I know that 1 and the number itself are factors, so I add them right away. Then, I use a `for` loop to go up to the square root of the number. This is a slight optimization; if you harvest the factors in pairs, you only have to search up to the square root.

As it stands, this is just a blob of code. How would it look different if TDD were used? The first test should be almost insanely simple. Here, I just want to get the factors for 1:

```
@Test public void factors_for_1() {
    int[] expected = new int[] {1};
    Classifier c = new Classifier(1);
    assertThat(c.getFactors(), is(expected));
}
```

I'm using JUnit 4.4 with the Hamcrest[*] matchers (Hamcrest matchers provide more English-friendly syntax for matchers, such as `assertThat(expected, is(c.getFactors()))`). How can this be a useful test? It seems too simple. Really simple tests like this aren't really about testing, they are about getting the infrastructure set up correctly. I must have the test libraries on the classpath, I need a class named `Classifier`, and I must resolve all the package dependencies. That's a lot of work! Writing a stupidly simple test allows me to get all the structure established before I have to start thinking about testing the actual hard problems.

Once I get this test to pass, I enhance it a little to make it look more like the expected real tests, changing it to a resizable list via a `List<Integer>`:

```
@Test public void factors_for_1() {
    List<Integer> expected = new ArrayList<Integer>(1);
    expected.add(1);
    Classifier c = new Classifier(1);
    assertThat(c.getFactors(), is(expected));
}
```

Once I get this test to pass, should I keep it around? Yes! I call these really simple tests *canary tests*. Just as miners took canaries into coal mines to warn of encroaching gas, this test performs a constant reality check for your tests. If it ever fails, you have serious problems with the infrastructure of your code: a JAR file has gotten misplaced, the code itself has moved, etc. These very simple tests can tell you if something fundamental has broken.

[*] Download at *http://code.google.com/p/hamcrest/*.

The next test I want to undertake checks for real factors of a number:

```java
@Test public void factors_for_6() {
    List<Integer> expected = new ArrayList<Integer>(
        Arrays.asList(1, 2, 3, 6));
    Classifier c = new Classifier(6);
    assertThat(c.getFactors(), is(expected));
}
```

This is the test I want to write, but it represents lots of different functionality: to make this test pass, I must know if a number is a factor, how to calculate factors, and how to harvest the factors I've found. This happens frequently during the TDD process: one test reveals lots of desired functionality. The best way to attack this daunting pile of work is to step back and think about what it takes to make this test a reality. By drilling down, I create the following tests (and the corresponding code to make them pass):

```java
@Test public void is_factor() {
    assertTrue(Classifier.isFactor(1, 10));
    assertTrue(Classifier.isFactor(5, 25));
    assertFalse(Classifier.isFactor(6, 25));
}

@Test public void add_factors() {
    Classifier c = new Classifier(20);
    c.addFactor(2);
    c.addFactor(4);
    c.addFactor(5);
    c.addFactor(10);
    List<Integer> expectation = new ArrayList<Integer>(
            Arrays.asList(1, 2, 4, 5, 10, 20));
    assertThat(c.getFactors(), is(expectation));
}
```

For the Classifier population code, 1 and the number itself (20) are added automatically, so I add the remaining factors. The first test is fine, but the second test fails after I implement the code in Classifier to populate the ArrayList:

```
java.lang.AssertionError: Expected: is <[1, 2, 4, 5, 10, 20] got: <[1, 20, 2, 10, 4, 5]>
```

The unexpected result stems from harvesting my numbers in pairs. This raises a fundamental question: should I add code to my Classifier to prevent duplication, or am I using the wrong abstraction? Factors have no inherent order, they are really a set. That indicates that I should change my Classifier to use a HashSet instead of an ArrayList. TDD excels at helping find mistaken assumptions early, where the pain of refactoring is small because there isn't much code yet. One interesting side note to the testing example: the addFactor() method is actually private in Classifier. I show how to test these kinds of private methods in "Java and Reflection" in Chapter 12.

Following this process through to its logical conclusion yields the following implementation of Classifier:

```java
public class Classifier {
    private int _number;
    private Set<Integer> _factors;
```

```java
    public Classifier(int number) {
        if (number < 0) throw new InvalidNumberException();
        setNumber(number);
    }

    public Classifier() {}

    public Set<Integer> getFactors() {
        return _factors;
    }

    public boolean isPerfect() {
        return sumOfFactorsFor(_number) - _number == _number;
    }

    public void calculateFactors() {
        for (int i = 2; i < Math.sqrt(_number) + 1; i++)
            addFactor(i);
    }

    private void addFactor(int i) {
        if (isFactor(i)) {
            _factors.add(i);
            _factors.add(_number / i);
        }
    }

    private int sumOfFactorsFor(int number) {
        calculateFactors();
        int sum = 0;
        for (int i : _factors)
            sum += i;
        return sum;
    }

    private boolean isFactor(int factor) {
        return _number % factor == 0;
    }

    public int getNumber() {
        return _number;
    }

    public void setNumber(int value) {
        _number = value;
        _factors = new HashSet<Integer>();
        _factors.add(1);
        _factors.add(_number);
    }
}
```

Measurements

If you compare the TDD version of the code to the non-TDD version, you'll see that the TDD one has much more code, but in lots of really small methods. Lots of small methods are good. If you read the method names, you will get a strong sense of the atomic operations required to compute perfect numbers. In fact, if you look at the comments in the original code, the same functionality (plus some) will show up as methods in the TDD version.

In six months, when it comes time to alter this code, you can make changes with confidence. If something breaks, you will know within a few lines of code what's wrong. The method names in TDD code describe an atomic operation, so when a test fails, you understand what you've broken more quickly. When dealing with code that has much longer methods, narrowing down to the errors takes much longer because you have to understand the context of the entire method before you can make changes to it. Understanding a three-line method shouldn't take any time at all. If you find yourself writing embedded comments within methods, your method should be more refined. Long methods with lots of comments reek of a noncomposed solution. Refactor the comments to methods to get rid of them.

NOTE
Refactor comments to methods.

One of the (few) useful code metrics is McCabe's Cyclomatic Complexity (see the next sidebar "Cyclomatic Complexity"). The average cyclomatic complexity for the PerfectNumberFinder class (the first, non-TDD version) is 5 (which is the cyclomatic complexity for the lone method, thus the average for the class). The TDD version scores a class average cyclomatic complexity of 1.5, which indicates that its methods (and therefore the class) are much simpler.

CYCLOMATIC COMPLEXITY

Thomas McCabe created the code metric called Cyclomatic Complexity to measure the complexity of code. The formula is quite simple: the number of edges – the number of nodes + 2, where the edges represent the execution path and nodes represent lines of code. For example, consider the following:

```
public void doit() {
    if (c1) {
        f1();
    } else {
        f2();
    }
    if (c2) {
        f3();
    } else {
        f4();
    }
}
```

If you graph this method like a flow chart (see Figure 6-1), you'll discover 8 edges and 7 nodes, meaning that this code has a cyclomatic complexity of 3.

Many tools exist to determine cyclomatic complexity (see Chapter 7 for some open source ones), including the analysis menus in the IntelliJ IDE.

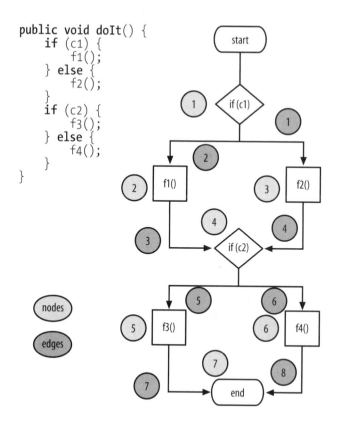

```
public void doIt() {
    if (c1) {
        f1();
    } else {
        f2();
    }
    if (c2) {
        f3();
    } else {
        f4();
    }
}
```

FIGURE 6-1. Determining cyclomatic complexity with a flow chart

Design Impact

Design impact is one last indicator of the design benefits of TDD. Let's say that your insatiable users pop up and decide that they want not only a perfect number finder, but one that calculates abundant numbers (numbers whose factors sum to more than the number) and deficient numbers (numbers whose factors sum to less than the number). In the first version of the perfect number finder, you'd have to go on a massive refactoring expedition, breaking it apart into something resembling the second version. And for the TDD version? Just add two methods:

```
public boolean isDeficient() {
    return sumOfFactorsFor(_number) - _number < _number;
}

public boolean isAbundant() {
    return sumOfFactorsFor(_number) - _number > _number;
}
```

All the building blocks already exist. TDD code tends to have more reusable elements because it forces you to write ultra-cohesive methods, and cohesive methods are the building blocks for truly reusable code.

TDD improves the design of your code, providing the following benefits:

- It forces consumption awareness in your code because you create the first consumer before you create any code.

- Testing (and keeping the tests) for extremely trivial initial cases provides warnings when you've accidentally broken critical infrastructure.

- Testing edge cases and boundary conditions is essential. Things that are difficult to test should either be refactored into simpler things, or, if you can't simplify them, they should be rigorously tested, no matter how hard it is. Complex things need testing the most!

- Always keep all your tests as part of your build process. The most insidious things in software are the side-effect faults that you accidentally introduce when making changes to a completely unrelated chunk of code. Running your unit tests as regression tests allows you to find those side effects immediately. Having this safety net of unit tests always saves you time and effort.

- Having a strong set of unit tests allows you to play "what if" refactoring games (that is, you can make a broad change and run your tests to determine the impact). When I first started working with developers who were accustomed to having strong unit tests, they would start making changes to the code, which made me nervous because wholesale changes can break lots of stuff. But they would do it at the drop of a hat, and I eventually came around when I realized that having tests gives you confidence to make changes that improve your code.

Code Coverage

One last really important testing topic is *code coverage*, which refers to the lines and branches executed in your code by tests. Open source and commercial code coverage tools exist for virtually every language.

For compiled languages (like Java and C#), code coverage works by first running an instrumentation processor on your compiled byte code. You then run your suite of unit tests against the instrumented code, which measures which lines are executed. The details are written to some intermediate form, from which a report is generated, showing the line and branch coverage of your tests. This is summarized in Figure 6-2.

The process is slightly different for dynamic languages, but the end result is the same: a report on how much of your code has been exercised by your tests. The report appears in your IDE, or in an XML or HTML view.

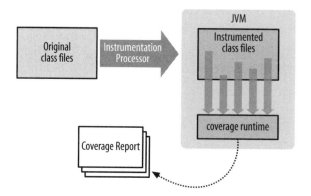

FIGURE 6-2. How code coverage works

This metric is critical because it tells you what has not been tested. Testing is the engineering rigor of software, and untested code is most likely where bugs live. If you are religious about TDD, all your code will be tested automatically, except for unusual fringe cases (for which you should add tests).

A lot of developers ask what the acceptable level of code coverage is. I used to be sanguine about this number, setting the acceptable threshold at about 80 percent. Then I noticed an interesting phenomenon: accepting only 80 percent coverage meant that the code that needed testing the most didn't get tests. Even conscientious developers write some complex code, run the code coverage report, and say "Whew! 82.3 percent. I wasn't looking forward to figuring out how to test that beast!"

I've come to the conclusion that anything less than 100 percent code coverage is a dangerous compromise. If you hold yourself to that highest standard, you will never have any code that's "too complex to test." You must write simpler code and when you encounter a truly complex scenario, you will be forced to come up with innovative ways to test it. Knowing that you don't have a "get out of testing free" card will make you more diligent about code hygiene.

But what if you already have a large code base that has no tests? It is wildly impractical to imagine that you can stop active development for months just to shore up your code coverage. First, set a date, somewhere in the near future (like next Thursday). Then, get the entire development team to agree that, after the inception date, your code coverage will always increase. That means that:

- All new code gets unit tests with 100 percent coverage (hopefully developed by TDD).
- Every time you fix a bug, you write a test.

It takes a great deal of effort to achieve 100 percent code coverage. You will write tests for all new code (which keeps it simpler), and you will write tests when you find bugs, meaning that the likelihood of bugs will diminish.

Like I just said, 100 percent code coverage on unit tests is a hard standard to achieve. However, I've been on projects that manage it, and it invariably improves the objective characteristics of the code (measured using static analysis and other measures; see Chapter 7).

CHAPTER SEVEN

Static Analysis

IF YOU ARE USING A STATICALLY TYPED LANGUAGE (LIKE JAVA OR C#), YOU HAVE AT YOUR
disposal a powerful way to isolate and find categories of bugs that are very difficult to find with code reviews and other traditional means. *Static analysis* is a programmatic validation mechanism where tools look for known bug patterns in your code.

Static analysis tools fall into two broad categories: those that look at compiled artifacts (that is, class files or byte code) and those that analyze source files. I give examples of each in this chapter, and I use Java because it has a very rich set of free static analysis tools. However, this technique is not restricted to Java code; tools exist for all major statically typed languages.

Byte Code Analysis

Byte code analyzers look for known bug patterns in compiled code. This implies two things. First, some languages have been studied enough to find common bug patterns in the compiled byte code. Second, these tools can't find arbitrary bugs—they find only bugs for which patterns have been defined. This doesn't mean that these tools are weak. Some of the bugs they find are extraordinarily difficult to find using other means (that is, by spending many unproductive hours staring at a debugger).

One such tool is FindBugs, an open source project from the University of Maryland. FindBugs operates in several different modes: command line, from an Ant task, and from a graphical environment. The FindBugs GUI appears in Figure 7-1.

FIGURE 7-1. The FindBugs graphical client

FindBugs finds bugs in several categories:

Correctness
> Indicates probable bug

Bad practice
> Violation of some recommended and essential coding practice (for example, overriding the `equals()` method but failing to also override the `hashCode()` method)

Dodgy
> Confusing code, odd usages, anomalies, poorly written code

To illustrate FindBugs, I had to choose a victim, so I downloaded the open source Struts web framework and ran FindBugs against it. It discovered some (probably) false positives in the "bad practice" category under the violation named "Equals method should not assume anything about the type of its argument." In Java, the recommended best practice when defining an `equals()` method is to check the lineage of the object passed to the method to make sure that an equals comparison makes sense. This is the offending code in Struts, in the file *ApplicationMap.java*:

```
entries.add(new Map.Entry() {
    public boolean equals(Object obj) {
        Map.Entry entry = (Map.Entry) obj;

        return ((key == null) ? (entry.getKey() == null) :
            key.equals(entry.getKey())) && ((value == null) ?
                (entry.getValue() == null) :
                value.equals(entry.getValue())));
    }
```

The reason I flag this as a potential false positive relates to the fact that this is an anonymous inner class definition, and perhaps the author always knows the argument types. It is a bit fishy, though.

Here's a bug that FindBugs uncovered that isn't open to debate. The following snippet of code appears in *IteratorGeneratorTag.java*:

```
if (countAttr != null && countAttr.length() > 0) {
        Object countObj = findValue(countAttr);
        if (countObj instanceof Integer) {
            count = ((Integer)countObj).intValue();
        }
        else if (countObj instanceof Float) {
            count = ((Float)countObj).intValue();
        }
        else if (countObj instanceof Long) {
            count = ((Long)countObj).intValue();
        }
        else if (countObj instanceof Double) {
            count = ((Long)countObj).intValue();
        }
```

Look closely at the last line of the listing. This falls under the FindBugs "correctness" category, with a violation called "Impossible cast." The last line of code above will always generate a class cast exception. In fact, there is no scenario under which you can run it that won't cause a problem. The developer verifies that countObj is of type Double, then immediately turns around and typecasts it as a Long. If you look at the previous if statement, you can see exactly what happened: a copy and paste error. This is the type of error that is hard to find in a code review because you'll tend to look right over it. Clearly, the Struts code base doesn't have a unit test that touches this line of code or it would have revealed itself immediately. What's worse, this particular error appears three times in the Struts code base: in the aforementioned *IteratorGeneratorTag.java* and twice in *SubsetIteratorTag.java*. The reason? You guessed it. The same chunk of code is copied and pasted in all three places. (FindBugs didn't figure that out— I just noticed that the offending code looked suspiciously similar.)

Because you can automate the execution of FindBugs via Ant or Maven as part of your build process, it becomes a very cheap insurance policy to find the bugs it knows about. It won't guarantee defect-free code (and it doesn't absolve you from writing unit tests), but it can find some nasty bugs for you. It can even find bugs that are hard to expose via unit testing, like thread synchronization problems.

> **NOTE**
> Static analysis tools represent cheap verification.

Source Analysis

As the name implies, source analysis tools look at your source code, searching for bug patterns. The tool I used in the following code is PMD, an open source tool for Java. PMD offers a command-line version, Ant support, and plug-ins for all major development environments. It looks for problems in the following categories:

Possible bugs
　　For example, empty try...catch blocks

Dead code
　　Unused local variables, parameters, and private variables

Suboptimal code
　　Wasteful string usage

Overcomplicated expressions
　　"Reuse" via copy and paste

Duplicate code (supported by an ancillary tool called CPD)
　　"Reuse" via copy and paste

PMD falls somewhere between pure style checkers (like CheckStyle, which makes sure that your code adheres to certain style guidelines like indentation) and FindBugs, which looks at byte code. As an example of the kinds of errors for which PMD excels, consider this Java method:

```
private void insertLineItems(ShoppingCart cart, int orderKey) {
    Iterator it = cart.getItemList().iterator();
    while (it.hasNext()) {
```

```
            CartItem ci = (CartItem) it.next();
            addLineItem(connection, orderKey, ci.getProduct().getId(),
                ci.getQuantity());
        }
    }
```

PMD will flag this method as improvable by making the first parameter (`ShoppingCart cart`) `final`. By making the parameter `final`, you allow the compiler to do more work for you. Because all objects are passed by value in Java, it is impossible to assign a new object reference to `cart` within the method, and attempting to do so indicates an error. PMD offers several clues like this that make existing tools (like the compiler) operate more efficiently.

PMD also comes with CPD, the Cut-Paste Detector, which scans your source code for suspiciously duplicated code (like copied and pasted code in Struts). CPD has a Swing-based user interface, showing status and offending code, as shown in Figure 7-2. This, of course, relates directly back to the DRY principle discussed in Chapter 5.

Most similar analysis tools offer customization APIs, allowing you to create your own rule sets (FindBugs and PMD both have such APIs). They also generally give you an interactive mode and, even more valuable, a way to run them as part of an automation process, like continuous integration. Running these tools upon every check-in of your code provides an extremely cheap way to avoid easy bugs. Someone has already done the hard work of identifying the bugs, and you get to reap the benefits.

Generate Metrics with Panopticode

The subject of metrics is beyond the scope of this book, but being *productive* about generating metrics is fair game. For static languages (like Java and C#), I'm a big fan of continuous metrics-gathering to make sure that problem resolution can happen as quickly as possible. Typically, that means that I have a set of metrics tools (including FindBugs and PMD/CPD) that I want to run as part of continuous integration.

It's a hassle having to wire up all that stuff for every project. As with Buildix (see "Don't Reinvent Wheels" in Chapter 4), I'd like to have all the infrastructure preconfigured. That's where Panopticode shines.

One of my colleagues (Julias Shaw) had the same problem, but instead of just complaining about it (like me), he fixed it. Panopticode[*] is an open source project with lots of common metrics tools preconfigured. The essence of Panopticode consists of an Ant build file with lots of open source projects and their JAR files preconfigured. You supply your source path, your library path (in other words, all the JAR files you need to build your project), and your test directory, then run Panopticode's build file. It does the rest.

---

[*] Download at *http://www.panopticode.org/*.

FIGURE 7-2. PMD's Cut and Paste Detector

Panopticode includes the following preconfigured metrics tools:

Emma
 Open source code coverage tool (see "Code Coverage" in Chapter 6). You can switch this
 to Cobertura (another open source code coverage tool for Java) with a single-line change
 within Panopticode's build file.

CheckStyle
 Open source code style verifier. You can supply your own custom rule sets with a single
 entry in Panopticode's build file.

JDepend
 Open source metrics tool that gathers numeric metrics at the package level.

JavaNCSS
 Open source cyclomatic complexity tool (see the sidebar "Cyclomatic Complexity" in
 Chapter 6).

Simian

A commercial code duplication finder. The version that comes with Panopticode has a 15-day license; you'll have to pay for it or remove it after that. Future plans are to make this interchangeable with CPD.

Panopticode Aggregator

Panopticode reports that show you the results of all these metrics in both textual and graphical form, using tree maps.

When you run Panopticode, it chews away at your code for a while, then produces reports reflecting the metrics results on your code. It also produces very nice *tree maps*, which are sophisticated scaled vector graphics (SVG) images (most modern browsers will display SVG files). The tree maps give you two things: first, a graphical overview of the value of a particular metric. The tree map shown in Figure 7-3 shows the cyclomatic complexity of the CruiseControl project. The shaded areas each show a different value range for the particular method. The thick white dividing lines show package boundaries, and the thinner ones show class boundaries. Each box represents a method.

The second benefit of the tree map is interactivity. This isn't just a pretty picture: it is interactive. When you display this tree map in a browser, when you click on one of the boxes, it shows you the metrics for that particular method on the righthand side. These tree maps allow you to analyze your code and find out exactly what classes and methods represent trouble.

Panopticode provides two great services. First, you don't have to configure all the same stuff over and over again for each project. If you have a pretty typical project structure, you can set up Panopticode in about five minutes. The graphical tree maps are the second benefit because they make great *information radiators*. In agile projects, an information radiator represents important project status placed in a conspicuous location (like near the coffee machine). Members of the team don't have to open an email attachment to find out project status: they accidentally find out as they go for coffee.

One of the tree maps Panopticode produces shows code coverage (again see "Code Coverage" in Chapter 6). Having a giant black blob representing your code coverage is depressing. When you start your initiative to increase code coverage, find the biggest color printer you can and print out the tree map for code coverage (actually, for most projects, a black and white printer will do for the first printout because it'll be all black anyway). Hang it in a conspicuous location. Once you reach a milestone where you've started writing tests, print out the latest version and hang it beside the first. The tree map becomes an unavoidable motivator for your developers: no one wants to see it slip back to the evil black days of yore. It also provides a nice, concise way to show your manager that your code is getting more code coverage. Managers like big, splashy graphics. And this one isn't information-free!

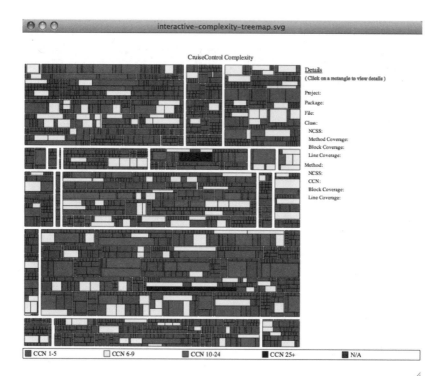

FIGURE 7-3. *Panopticode's tree map of CruiseControl's cyclomatic complexity*

Analysis for Dynamic Languages

While dynamic languages are considered more productive in many development scenarios, they lack the kinds of analysis tools that exist for statically typed languages. Building analysis tools for dynamic languages is more difficult because you don't have the characteristics of the type system to lean upon.

Most of the efforts in the dynamic language world center around cyclomatic complexity (which is universal in virtually every block-based language) and code coverage. For example, in the Ruby world, rcov is a commonly used code coverage tool. In fact, Ruby on Rails comes with rcov preconfigured (you can see an rcov report in Figure 15-1). For cyclomatic complexity, you can use the open source Saikuro.†

---

† Download at *http://saikuro.rubyforge.org/*.

Because of the lack of "traditional" static analysis tools, Ruby developers have gotten clever. A couple of interesting projects have emerged to measure code quality in nontraditional ways. The first is flog.‡ Flog measures ABC: assignments, branches, and calls, with added weight on calls. Flog assigns a weighted value to each line of a method and reports the results like this (this is a run of flog on the `SqlSplitter` example in "Refactoring SqlSplitter for Testablility" in Chapter 15):

```
SqlSplitter#generate_sql_chunks: (32.4)
    20.8: assignment
     7.0: branch
     3.4: downcase
     3.0: +
     2.9: ==
     2.8: create_output_file_from_number
     2.8: close
     2.0: lit_fixnum
     1.7: %
     1.4: puts
     1.4: lines_o_sql
     1.2: each
     1.2: make_a_place_for_output_files
SqlSplitter#create_output_file_from_number: (11.2)
     4.8: +
     3.0: |
     1.8: to_s
     1.2: assignment
     1.2: new
     0.4: lit_fixnum
```

This result indicates that the `generate_sql_chunks` method is the most complex in the class with a score of 32.4, derived from the values listed below it. The highest complexity in the method revolves around assignments. Thus, to simplify this code you should attack the myriad assignments in the method first.

Groovy is a special case because it is a dynamic language that produces Java byte code. This means that you can run the standard Java static analysis tools provided they work against the byte code. However, the results might not be satisfactory. Because Groovy must create lots of proxy and wrapper classes to work some of its magic, you will get lots of references to classes you didn't actually create. The developers of metrics tools for Java have started taking Groovy into account (for example, the Cobertura code coverage tool is now Groovy-friendly), but it is still early.

---

‡ Download at *http://ruby.sadi.st/Flog.html.*

CHAPTER EIGHT

Good Citizenship

GOOD CITIZENSHIP MAY SEEM LIKE AN ODD TOPIC IN A DISCUSSION ABOUT HOW TO IMPROVE code, but good citizenship refers to objects that are both aware of their own state and considerate of the state of others around them. Although this may seem simple, developers violate this principle all the time by coding on autopilot. This chapter looks at several different violators of good citizenship and ways to become more responsible citizens.

Breaking Encapsulation

One of the core tenets of object-oriented programming is *encapsulation*: protecting internal fields from outside meddling. Yet, I've seen lots of developers void the intent of encapsulation because they code on autopilot.

Here is a scenario. You create a new class, you create a bunch of private member variables for it, you tell the IDE to spit out properties (either get/set methods in Java or properties in C#), and *then* you engage your brain. Creating public properties for every private field completely destroys the intent of the property mechanism. You might as well make all the member variables public because the properties aren't helping you at all (and, in fact, they are just making your code more dense for no good reason).

For example, let's say you have a Customer class that has several address fields (such as the typical addressLine, city, state, zip). If you create mutating properties for each of these fields, you open the door for someone to make your Customer a bad citizen, meaning that it has an invalid state. It doesn't make sense in the real world for customers to have incomplete addresses. Generally, they either have a complete address or nothing. Don't let your code put your customer object (which is supposed to reflect the real-world customer) into a state that doesn't make sense for your business. The read-only properties are probably OK, but you should create an atomic mutator instead of providing one for each field:

```
class Customer {
    private String _adrLine;
    private String _city;
    private String _state;
    private String _zip;

    public void addAddress(String adrLine, String city,
            String state, String zip) {
        _adrLine = adrLine;
        _city    = city;
        _state   = state;
        _zip     = zip;
    }
}
```

Having an atomic mutator means that your object moves from one known legal state to another known legal state in one step. This has a couple of benefits. First, it means that you can skip validation code later to make sure you have a valid address. If you can never create an invalid address, you don't have to guard against it. Second, it makes your customer abstraction match more closely to the real customer you model. As the real customer changes, your code can change along with it because they are so semantically close.

Instead of blindly creating properties when you create a new class, here is an alternative strategy: create properties only when you need to call them from other code. This serves several purposes. First, you don't have any code you don't actually need. Developers create far too much speculative code because they think "I'm sure I'll need that later, might as well create it now." Because you are letting the tool create properties for you anyway, it's no more work to create them as you need them than to create them up front. Second, you cut down on needless code bloat. Properties take up lots of space in source files, and reading through all that boilerplate code slows you down. Third, you don't have to worry about writing unit tests for your properties. Because you are always calling them from some other method that utilizes the property, they will automatically get code coverage in your tests. I never do test-driven development for properties (get/set methods in Java, properties in C#); instead, I allow them to come into being only when there is a real need.

Constructors

In most modern object-oriented languages, we take constructors for granted. We think of them merely as the mechanism used to create new objects. But constructors have a more noble purpose: they tell you what it takes to create a valid object of a certain type. Constructors form a contractual relationship with the consumers of an object, indicating what fields must be populated in order to have a valid object of this type.

Unfortunately, the authorities in the language worlds advocate against having meaningful constructors. Most languages virtually insist that all classes have a default constructor (that is, one that takes no parameters). From a citizenship standpoint, this doesn't make any sense. How many times have you heard one of the business people say, "We need to ship widgets to this customer, but we don't have any information about it." You can't ship things to customers that have no internal state. Objects are the keepers of state, and having an object with no state doesn't make sense. Virtually every object should start out with at least some minimal initial state. Is it possible in your company to have a customer that doesn't have a name?

Pushing back on default constructors is hard. Many frameworks insist on them and get angry if you don't supply them. The "must have a default constructor" rule is even codified in Java, in the JavaBeans specification. If a framework or language standard forces the issue, it will win (unless you can replace it with a friendlier one). In that case, treat the default constructor as an anomaly, like the ugly serialization cruft you must sometimes attach to your domain objects.

Static Methods

Static methods have one wonderful use: as a black-box, standalone, stateless method. The use of static methods of the `Math` class in Java illustrates good use. When you call the `Math.sqrt()`

method, you don't worry that a subsequent call might return the cube root instead of the square root because some state within the sqrt() method changed. Static methods work well when they are completely stateless. You get into trouble when you start mixing staticness and state.

STATIC METHODS AND HAWAII

For many years, I worked at a consulting and training company, and we taught a wide variety of Java topics. I got what was considered the Holy Grail of teaching gigs: two classes to two groups of developers in Hawaii. The schedule had me there two weeks (one week per class), three weeks back home, and then there again for the second set of classes for two weeks. And, of course, I was required to stay over the weekend, and as a good company man, I managed to persevere. It was a tough class, however, because all of the students came from a mainframe background. I remember one student who couldn't quite grasp the concept of matching curly braces and thought that all compilation errors meant that you needed to add more curly braces at the end of the file. I would go to help this person and there would be a dozen close braces, all on one line.

Anyway, I struggled through and returned three weeks later for the second part of the class. I was greeted immediately by one of the students who proudly exclaimed, "While you were gone, we figured out Java!" I was shocked and wanted to see what kind of code they had been writing. Then she showed me. All the code looked pretty much like this:

```
public static Hashtable updateCustomer(
        Hashtable customerInfo, Hashtable newInfo) {
    customerInfo.put("name", newInfo.get("name"));
    // . . .
}
```

They had achieved what I thought impossible: they had turned Java into a procedural language! With loose variable typing, no less. Needless to say, I spent the next weeks teaching them how *not* to use Java in this way.

This ancedote illustrates how the overuse of static methods indicates a procedural mindset. If you find yourself with lots of static methods, question the correctness of your abstractions.

The common evil combination of "static" and "state" occurs with the singleton design pattern. The goal of singleton is to create a class that can be instantiated only once. All subsequent attempts to create an instance of the class return the original instance. Singleton is typically implemented like this (the following is Java code, but it looks pretty much the same in virtually every language):

```
public class ConfigSingleton {
    private static ConfigSingleton myInstance;
    private Point _initialPosition;

    public Point getInitialPosition() {
```

```
            return _initialPosition;
        }

        private ConfigSingleton() {
            Dimension screenSize =
                    Toolkit.getDefaultToolkit().getScreenSize();
            _initialPosition = new Point();
            _initialPosition.x = (int) screenSize.getWidth() / 2;
            _initialPosition.y = (int) screenSize.getHeight() / 2;
        }

        public static ConfigSingleton getInstance() {
            if (myInstance == null)
                myInstance = new ConfigSingleton();
            return myInstance;
        }
    }
```

In this listing, the getInstance() method checks to see if one already exists, creates the sole instance if needed, then returns the reference to it. Note that this method isn't thread safe, but this topic isn't about thread safety and it just adds more complexity. The thing that's so evil about singleton is the embedded state, which makes it untestable. Unit testing manipulates state, but there is no way to manipulate the state of this singleton object. Because construction is atomic in Java, there is no way you can test this class with any value of initialPosition rather than the constructed value derived from the current screen size. A singleton is the object-oriented version of a global variable, and everyone knows that global variables are bad.

NOTE
Don't create global variables, even the object kind.

Ultimately, what makes singleton so smelly is the fact that you have a single class that has two distinct responsibilities: policing the instances of itself and providing configuration information. Any time you have a single class with multiple unrelated responsibilities, you have a code smell.

But it's useful to have only a single configuration object. How can you achieve that without using a singleton? You can use a plain object plus a factory, delegating the individual responsibilities to each. The factory is responsible for the instance policing and the plain object (POJO in Java speak) deals only with configuration information and behavior.

Here is the updated configuration object as a POJO:

```
public class Configuration {
    private Point _initialPosition;

    private Configuration(Dimension screenSize) {
        _initialPosition = new Point();
        _initialPosition.x = (int) screenSize.getWidth() / 2;
        _initialPosition.y = (int) screenSize.getHeight() / 2;
    }

    public int getInitialX() {
        return _initialPosition.x;
    }
```

```
        public int getInitialY() {
            return _initialPosition.y;
        }
    }
```

This class is trivial to test. Both the unit test and factory will use reflection to create the class. In Java, private access is little more than documentation indicating suggested usage. In modern languages, you can always bypass it with reflection if the need arises. This represents a good case where you don't expect anyone to instantiate one of these classes; therefore, the constructor is private.

The following listing shows the unit tests for this class, including the instantiation via reflection and accessing the private field via reflection to test the class's behavior with different values:

```
public class TestConfiguration {
    Configuration c;

    @Before public void setUp() {❶
        try {
            Constructor cxtor[] =
                    Configuration.class.getDeclaredConstructors();
            cxtor[0].setAccessible(true);
            c = (Configuration) cxtor[0].newInstance(
                    Toolkit.getDefaultToolkit().getScreenSize());
        } catch (Throwable e) {
            fail();
        }
    }

    @Test
    public void initial_position_set_correctly_upon_instantiation() {
        Configuration specialConfig = null;
        Dimension screenSize = null;
        try {
            Constructor cxtor[] =
                    Configuration.class.getDeclaredConstructors();
            cxtor[0].setAccessible(true);
            screenSize = new Dimension(26, 26);
            specialConfig = (Configuration) cxtor[0].newInstance(screenSize);
        } catch (Throwable e) {
            fail();
        }

        Point expected = new Point();
        expected.x = (int) screenSize.getWidth() / 2;
        expected.y = (int) screenSize.getHeight() / 2;
        assertEquals(expected.x, specialConfig.getInitialX());
        assertEquals(expected.y, specialConfig.getInitialY());
    }

    @Test
    public void initial_postion_can_be_changed_after_instantiation() {
        Field f = null;
        try {
            f = Configuration.class.getDeclaredField("_initialPosition");❷
            f.setAccessible(true);
            f.set(c, new Point(10, 10));
        } catch (Throwable t) {
            fail();
        }
```

```
            Assert.assertEquals(10, c.getInitialX());
    }
}
```

❶ The setUp() method creates the Configuration object via reflection and calls initialize() to create a valid object for most of the tests.

❷ You can access the private field _initialPosition using reflection to see what would happen in your configuration class if the initial position is something other than the default.

Making the Configuration class a plain object ensures that it is easy to test and doesn't compromise any of the functionality it had before.

The factory responsible for creating configuration is also simple and testable; the code for ConfigurationFactory appears here:

```
public class ConfigurationFactory {
    private static Configuration myConfig;

    public static Configuration getConfiguration() {
        if (myConfig == null) {
            try {
                Constructor cxtor[] =
                    Configuration.class.getDeclaredConstructors();
                cxtor[0].setAccessible(true);
                myConfig = (Configuration) cxtor[0].newInstance(
                    Toolkit.getDefaultToolkit().getScreenSize());
            } catch (Throwable e) {
                throw new RuntimeException("can't construct Configuration");
            }
        }
        return myConfig;
    }
}
```

Not surprisingly, this code looks just like the creation code from the original singleton. The important difference is that this code does only one thing: police the instances of the Configuration class. The ConfigurationFactory is also very testable, as shown here:

```
public class TestConfigurationFactory {

    @Test
    public void creation_creates_a_single_instance() {
        Configuration config1 = ConfigurationFactory.getConfiguration();
        assertNotNull(config1);
        Configuration config2 = ConfigurationFactory.getConfiguration();
        assertNotNull(config2);
        assertSame(config1, config2);
    }
}
```

Static methods offer yet one more pitfall: Java allows you to call them via object instances, which can cause confusion because you can't override static methods. Java doesn't warn you in any way that you are calling a static method using an object (not the class) as the receiver. Static methods also cause confusion when mixed with base and derived types and can be called in confusing ways. Consider this code:

```
Derived d = new Derived();
Base b = d;
int x = d.getNumber();
int y = b.getNumber();
int z = ((Base)(null)).getNumber();
System.out.println("x = " + x + "\ty = "
                    + y + "\tz = " + z);
```

It assumes a Base class with a getNumber() method and a class named Derived that extends from Base. You can legally call the same getNumber() method in all the ways shown earlier.

While static methods offer some benefits, the number of pitfalls suggests that Java should have perhaps created a different mechanism that is not so rife with potential headaches.

Criminal Behavior

What happens when an antisocial criminal moves into the neighborhood? java.util.Calendar exhibits lots of hostile behavior toward the other citizens in the Java world. It allows engineering purity to override common sense. The constant values that define the months start counting from 0 (which is the standard in the rest of Java), meaning that if you pass the number 2 to set the month, it sets March. I understand the consistency of everything being numbered from 0, but it is insane to take a well-known association (month numbers) and override it.

Calendar also doesn't maintain its own internal state correctly. What happens when you execute the following code?

```
c = Calendar.getInstance();

c.set(Calendar.MONTH, Calendar.FEBRUARY);
c.set(Calendar.DATE, 31);

System.out.println(c.get(Calendar.MONTH));
System.out.println(c.get(Calendar.DATE));
```

The output is 2 and 2, which after decryption reveals that it believes that the proper date is March 2nd. You have told a calendar to set a date of February 31st, and it silently returns March 2nd. How many times do you tell your friend, "Meet me at the place on February 31st" and your friend says, "You mean March 2nd, right?" Calendar knows nothing about its internal state, allowing you to set dates that can never actually exist. Instead of complaining with an exception, it just silently gives you a completely different date. Objects are supposed to be the keepers of state, yet Calendar seems to know nothing about its state.

Why does Calendar act this way? The problem is the ability to set individual fields. You should be forced to perform atomic updates for the calendar, setting the month, date, and year at the same time, which would allow the calendar to validate that it has a real date for the current calendar. However, Calendar doesn't have that because the method signature would be immensely long. The reason for that? Calendar is tracking too much information. It keeps not only date information, but also time information. You'd have to set the date and the time of day, which would be an annoying method signature. When was the last time someone asked you the time and you said, "Hold on—I've got to check my calendar"? `Calendar` has far too much responsibility, harming both the object as the keeper of state and the usefulness of the class.

What does Neighborhood Watch do when it spots a criminal? Kick him out of the neighborhood! The open source Joda library is a saner calendar replacement.[*] Don't build classes that act as bad citizens and don't use them either. Trying to work around the quirks of broken things like `Calendar` will make all your code needlessly more complex.

---

[*] Download at *http://joda-time.sourceforge.net/*.

CHAPTER NINE

YAGNI

YAGNI STANDS FOR "YOU AIN'T GONNA NEED IT." It is the battle cry of agile project development to help prevent speculative development. Speculative development occurs when developers tell themselves, "I'm sure I'm going to need some additional functionality later, so I'll go ahead and write it now." This is a slippery slope. The better approach is to build only what you need right now.

Speculative development harms software because it adds complexity to code prematurely. As Andrew Hunt and David Thomas stated in *The Pragmatic Programmer* (Addison-Wesley), software suffers from *entropy*, which is a mathematical term for the amount of complexity in a system. Entropy hits software hard because complexity makes it hard to make changes, understand the code, and add new features. Usually, in the physical world, things tend toward simplicity unless you add energy to disrupt it. Software is the opposite: because it is so easy to create, it tends toward complexity (in other words, it takes the same physical effort to create both complex and simple software). It can take great effort to pull software back toward simplicity.

All developers fall into the gold plating trap. Speculative development is a hard habit to break. It's really hard when you are in the heat of development to be objective about the clever idea you just had. Will it make the code better, or just add more complexity? Incidentally, that is part of the effectiveness of pair-programming. Having someone else there who offers an objective viewpoint of your brilliant idea is invaluable. Developers have a hard time being objective about their own ideas, especially when those ideas are fresh.

Whatever form it takes, though, the health of your software suffers if you indulge in too much speculative development. In its worst form, it leads to *frameworks*! Frameworks aren't inherently bad, but they illustrate a symptom of the speculative development disease. Java has this disease worse than any other language. If you add up all the other frameworks in the development world, for all other technologies, Java still has more of them. Java even has meta-frameworks, which are frameworks that make it easy to build other frameworks. This insanity should stop!

Frameworks are only bad when they are built purely speculatively. A couple of classic examples exist in the Java world: Enterprise JavaBeans (EJB) (versions 1 & 2) and JavaServer Faces (JSF). Both are massively over-engineered, making it hard to use them to get real work done. EJB has become a cautionary tale of over-engineering because it was so complex and solved a problem that very few projects had. Yet, the conventional wisdom in the Java world at the time encouraged its use. The JSF case is a little different but just as illustrative. One of the "features" of JSF is its ability to have custom rendering pipelines, allowing you to generate not just HTML, but also WML (Wireless Markup Language), or even raw XML. I have yet to talk to a developer who has actually used these facilities, yet everyone who uses JSF pays some complexity tax for their presence. This is the classic example of ivory tower designers thinking up something cool and adding it to the framework. What's insidious is that it sounds cool to developers too, making the marketing effort easier. Yet, at the end of the day, a feature that you don't use just adds to the entropy of your software.

Don't pay complexity tax unless you absolutely must.

Frameworks aren't inherently bad. Quite the contrary: they have become the preferred abstraction style, achieving much of the promised code reuse of the object-oriented development and component movements. But, frameworks harm your project when they have significantly more functionality than you need because they inherently add complexity. The best frameworks do not come from ivory tower designers, trying to anticipate what developers need. The best frameworks are *extracted* from working code. Someone builds an actual working application. Then, when the time comes to build another application, the developer looks at what worked well in the first one, extracts that, and applies it to the second one. That is one of the reasons that the Ruby on Rails web framework has so little excess baggage. It was extracted from working code.

YAGNI isn't an admonition to never use frameworks, but an admission that they aren't silver bullets. Look at what the framework offers. If there is a significant overlap with what you need, it's certainly worth using it because it represents code you won't have to write yourself. On the other hand, if someone hands you an EJB framework, be suspicious.

DON'T SAY IT!

We had a small project where we needed to use .NET. As the tech lead, I didn't want to use a full-blown object-relational mapper (O/R mapper) such as nHibernate or iBatis.net because I didn't think the size of the project warranted it. However, using the raw database libraries of .NET was cumbersome because they are notoriously hard to unit test. I told the project manager that I wanted to build a very small framework around ADO.NET, offering just the functionality we would need, but testable. I thought the project manager was going to throw a fit. "Don't ever say the word *framework* around me!" he stormed. It turned out that he had worked on a project that ended up chasing the framework myth at the expense of delivering software, and he didn't want to go there again. But, being persistent (and the tech lead), I convinced him that it needed to be done.

Of course, he was right. I built the little framework (never saying the actual word around him), and we started the project. For the first couple of uses, the framework was great: we built what we needed really quickly and were able to test it. Then, the inevitable happened. One of the things we needed to build wasn't supported well in the framework, so I had to add some features. Then it happened again. Before long, I was spending half my time maintaining the framework, while the project manager fumed in the wings.

We ended up finishing the project on time. The time saved early on by my magical framework was paid back with interest by the end because adding functionality to the framework ate time. I thought I had considered all the things we would need, but it's just too hard in software to anticipate all the nuances of what will happen during a project. I apologized to the project manager. If I were doing it again, I would use the already functional frameworks like nHibernate or iBatis because we ended up building a small, buggy subset of what they offered in the first place.

Another source of YAGNI is *creeping featurism*, which attacks commercial software hard. The scenario goes something like this:

> Marketing: "We need X to sell against feature Y of competitor Z."
> Engineering: "Gee, do our customers really care about either X or Y?"
> Marketing: "Of course they do. That's why we're Marketing."
> Engineering: "OK."

This is a tough problem because Marketing thinks that they know what is best, and they probably do. However, they don't fully understand the impact of adding more complexity to software and that Feature A takes orders of magnitude longer to add than Feature B, which seems the same to the nondevelopers.

It is important to keep channels of communication open between the business drivers and developers. Always be willing to offer suggestions that meet the spirit of the request if not the actual details. Most of the time, users and business analysts have a particular vision in mind for how a feature should work. Try to get to the core of what the feature does, and see if a simpler solution exists. I've had very good success making alternative suggestions that were much easier to implement but that served the same business need. Communication is paramount: without good communication channels, you have constant frustration between the perceived pushy users and the overly reticent developers. Remember the lessons of the ship Vasa (see the next sidebar).

> **NOTE**
> Software development is first and foremost a communication game.

THE GOOD SHIP VASA

In 1625, King Gustav II Adolf of Sweden commissioned the finest warship ever built. He hired the best ship builder, grew a special forest of the mightiest oaks, and started work on the ship Vasa. The king kept making requests to make the ship grander and grander, with ornate decorations everywhere. At some point, he decided that he wanted a ship with two gun decks, unlike any in the world. His ship was going to be the most powerful in the ocean. And he needed it right away because of a diplomatic issue that was popping up. Of course, the ship builder had designed the ship with only one gun deck in mind, but because the king asked for it, he got his extra gun deck. Because they were in a rush, the builders didn't have time for "lurch" tests, where a group of sailors would run from one side to the other to make sure the ship didn't rock too much (in other words, wasn't too top heavy). On the inaugural voyage, the Vasa sank within a few hours. While adding all the "features" to the ship, they managed to make it unseaworthy. The Vasa sat at the bottom of the North Sea until early in the 20th century, when the well-preserved ship was raised and placed in a museum.

And here is the interesting question: whose fault was the sinking of the Vasa? The king, for asking for more and more features? Or the builders, who built what he wanted without vocalizing their concerns loudly enough? Look around at the project on which you are currently working: are you creating another Vasa?

Focus on adding capability instead of complexity to your software. Consider two code bases that have the same functionality. One was built with rigorous adherence to simplicity, applying YAGNI at every step of the way. The other was built with features that, while they aren't needed immediately, will probably have a legitimate use at some point in the future. However, with the second code base, you start paying for the extra features immediately in terms of refactorability, which in turn affects the rate of change you can make in the project. Features you don't yet need also make code harder to maintain and extend in legitimate ways. Volume matters in code. Keeping unused code out of your code base means you have less to wade through when you change the existing functional code. If features were weight, the comparison would look like Figure 9-1.

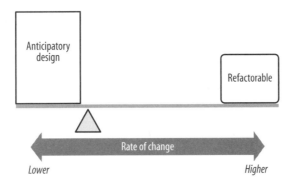

FIGURE 9-1. If features = weight, the relative ease of making changes to speculative development versus YAGNI code bases

Diligently building only what you need *right now* is hard, but in the end you will have a better code base. Complexity you don't add means complexity you don't have to slog through when you need to make legitimate changes or refactor your code. Keep in mind that entropy kills software, and add features as reluctantly as possible.

CHAPTER TEN

Ancient Philosophers

IT MAY SEEM ODD TO FIND A CHAPTER ABOUT ANCIENT PHILOSOPHERS IN A BOOK ABOUT programmer productivity, yet here it is. It turns out that some of the general discoveries made by ancient (and not so ancient) philosophers have direct bearing on building quality software. Let's see what a few philosophers have to say about code.

Aristotle's Essential and Accidental Properties

Aristotle founded many of the branches of science we know today. In fact, the study of science pretty much traces back to him. He categorized, cataloged, and defined entire fields of thought about the natural world. He also built the foundations of logic and formal thinking.

One of the logical principles Aristotle defined was the distinction between *essential* and *accidental* properties. Let's say you have a group of five bachelors, all of whom have brown eyes. Unmarriedness is the essential property of the group. Brown eyes is an accidental property. You can't make the logical deduction that all bachelors have brown eyes because the eye color is really just coincidental.

OK, so what does this have to do with software? Extending this concept a little further leads us to the idea of essential and accidental complexity. *Essential complexity* is the core of the problem we have to solve, and it consists of the parts of the software that are legitimately difficult problems. Most software problems contain some complexity. *Accidental complexity* is all the stuff that doesn't necessarily relate directly to the solution, but that we have to deal with anyway.

An example is in order. Let's say that the essential complexity of a problem is the tracking of customer data by placing it in a database from a web page—a nice, straightforward problem. But, to get it to work within your organization, you must use an old database that has spotty driver support. And, of course, you have to worry about getting permissions to access the database. Some of the database must be cross-checked with similar data that lives in a mainframe somewhere. Now, you have to find out how to connect to the mainframe and extract the data in a form that you can work with. It turns out that you can't get to the data directly because there is no connector technology from what you are using, so you must get someone to extract the data and put it in a data warehouse so that you can get to it. Does this sound like your job? The essential complexity description can be wrapped up in one sentence. The accidental complexity description could go on forever.

No one sets out to spend more time dealing with accidental complexity than essential complexity. But lots of organizations end up doing little more than servicing the accidental complexity layers that accrue over time. Much of the current fad for SOA (service-oriented architecture) derives from companies trying to mitigate the amount of accidental complexity that has built up over time. SOA is an architectural style that binds disparate applications together so that they can communicate. Very rarely would you ever define that problem as the driving force of your business. It is, however, exactly what you'd do if you had lots of uncommunicative applications around that needed to share information. Sounds like accidental complexity to me. The vendorization of the SOA architectural style is the Enterprise Service Bus (ESB), whose chief selling point seems to be that the solution to the problem of middleware is more middleware. Does adding complexity reduce complexity? Hardly. Be leery of vendor-driven solutions to every possible problem. Their first priority is to sell their product, and their second priority is (maybe) to make your life better.

Identification is the first step in ridding yourself of accidental complexity. Think about the processes, policies, and technical mazes with which you currently deal. Noticing what is essential may lead you toward abandoning something whose contribution to the real problem outweighs the amount of complexity it introduces to the overall problem. For example, you may think you need a data warehouse, but the amount of complexity it adds to the overall problem isn't worth the benefits it might provide. You can never kill all accidental complexity with software, but you can continually try to minimize it.

> NOTE
> Maximize work on essential complexity; kill accidental complexity.

Occam's Razor

Sir William of Occam was a monk who disdained ornate, elaborate explanations. His contribution to philosophy and science is known as Occam's Razor, which says that given multiple explanations for something, the simplest is the most likely. Obviously, this ties in nicely with our discussion of essential versus accidental complexity. How far into the software stack this goes, however, is surprising.

As an industry, we've been engaged in an experiment for the last decade or so. This experiment started back in the mid to late '90s, largely driven by the fact that the demand for software vastly outstripped the supply of people who could write it (this wasn't a new problem—it's been going on almost since the idea of business software started). The goal of the experiment: to create tools and environments that would allow average and/or mediocre developers to be productive, regardless of the messy facts already known by people like Fred Brooks (see his book *The Mythical Man-Month* [Addison-Wesley]). The reasoning was that if we could create languages that keep people out of trouble by restricting the damage they could do, we could produce software without having to pay those annoying software craftsmen ridiculous amounts of money (and you probably wouldn't be able to find enough of them even then). This thinking gave us tools like dBASE, PowerBuilder, Clipper, and Access—the rise of the 4GLs (4th Generation Languages), which include tool/language combinations like FoxPro and Access.

But the problem was that you couldn't get enough done in those environments. They created what my colleague Terry Dietzler called the "80-10-10 Rule" for Access (which I've renamed Dietzler's Law): you can do 80 percent of what the customer wants in a remarkably short time. The next 10 percent is possible, but takes a lot of effort. The last 10 percent is flat out impossible because you can't get "underneath" all the tooling and frameworks. And users want 100 percent of what they want, so 4GLs gave way to general-purpose languages (Visual BASIC, Java, Delphi, and eventually C#). Java and C# in particular were designed to make C++ easier and less error prone, so the developers built-in some fairly serious restrictions in the interest of keeping average developers out of trouble. They created their own versions of the "80-10-10 Rule," only this time the stuff you couldn't do was much more subtle. Because these languages are general-purpose languages, you can get pretty much anything done...with enough effort. Java kept bumping into stuff that would be nice to do but was way too much work, so frameworks were built. And built. And built. Aspects were added. More frameworks were built.

Here's an example. Consider the following Java code, extracted from a widely used open source framework. Try to figure out what it does (I'll show you the name of the method in just a bit):

```java
public static boolean xxXxxxx(String str) {
    int strLen;
    if (str == null || (strLen = str.length()) == 0) {
        return true;
    }
    for (int i = 0; i < strLen; i++) {
        if ((Character.isWhitespace(str.charAt(i)) == false)) {
            return false;
        }
    }
    return true;
}
```

How long did it take you? This is in fact the isBlank method, from the Jakarta Commons framework (which provides helper classes and methods that probably should have been built-in to Java). The definition of string blankness has two parts: the string is either empty or it is comprised of only spaces. This code is a very complex formula for those criteria because it has to consider the case of a null parameter, and iterate over all the characters. But, of course, you must use the Character type wrapper to find out if a given character is whitespace. Yuck!

Here is the same code in Ruby:

```ruby
class String
  def blank?
    empty? || strip.empty?
  end
end
```

This definition is pretty close to the written one earlier. In Ruby, you can open the String class and add new methods to it. The blank? method (Ruby methods that return Booleans traditionally end with a question mark) checks to see if the string is either empty or if it's empty if you remove all the spaces. The last line of a method in Ruby is the return value, so you can skip the optional return keyword.

This code works in unexpected places as well. Consider these unit tests for it:

```ruby
class BlankTest < Test::Unit::TestCase
  def test_blank
    assert "".blank?
    assert " ".blank?
    assert nil.to_s.blank?❶
```

```
        assert ! "x".blank?
    end
end
```

❶ In Ruby, nil is an instance of NilClass, meaning that it has a to_s method (Ruby's equivalent of the toString method in Java and C#).

The point is that the mainstream statically typed languages that are popular for "enterprise development" include lots of accidental complexity. Primitives in Java are a perfect example of accidental complexity in the language. Although useful when Java was brand new, now they just encrypt our code. Autoboxing helps some, but it leads to other unusual problems. Consider the following, which will surely have you scratching your head:

```
public void test_Compiler_is_sane_with_lists() {
    ArrayList<String> list = new ArrayList<String>();
    list.add("one");
    list.add("two");
    list.add("three");
    list.remove(0);
    assertEquals(2, list.size());
}
```

This code works as expected. But consider this version, which changes a single word from the previous example (ArrayList to Collection):

```
public void test_Compiler_is_broken_with_collections() {
    Collection<String> list = new ArrayList<String>();
    list.add("one");
    list.add("two");
    list.add("three");
    list.remove(0);
    assertEquals(2, list.size());
}
```

This test fails, complaining that the list size is still 3. What gives? This example illustrates what happens when you retrofit a complex library (like collections) with generics and autoboxing. The problem lies with the fact that the Collection interface has a remove method, but it removes the item matching the content, not the item in that index order. In this case, Java autoboxes the integer 2 into an Integer object, looks in the list to see if there is an element with the content of 2, fails to find one, and doesn't remove anything from the list.

Instead of keeping developers out of trouble, the accidental complexity of modern languages has forced developers to wade through lots of complicated workarounds. This trend has a negative impact on productivity when building complex software. What we really want is the productivity of 4GLs with the generality and flexibility of powerful general-purpose languages. Enter frameworks built with domain-specific languages (DSLs), the current exemplar being Ruby on Rails. When writing a Rails application, you don't write that much "pure" Ruby code (and most of that is in models, for business rules). Mostly, you are writing code in the DSL part of Rails. That means that you get major bang for the buck:

```
validates_presence_of :name, :sales_description, :logo_image_url
validates_numericality_of :account_balance
validates_uniqueness_of :name
validates_format_of :logo_image_url,
```

```
:with => %r{\.(gif|jpg|png)}i,
:message => "must be a URL for a GIF, JPG, or PNG image"
```

You get a ton of functionality with this little bit of code. It offers 4GL levels of productivity, but with a critical difference. In a 4GL (and the current mainstream statically typed languages), it is cumbersome or impossible to do really powerful stuff (like meta-programming). In a DSL written on *top* of a super-powerful language, you can drop one level of abstraction to the underlying language to do whatever you need to get done.

Powerful languages + domain-specific meta-layers offer the best approach currently available. The productivity comes from working close to the problem domain in the DSL; the power comes from the abstraction layer simmering just below the surface. Expressive DSLs on top of powerful languages will become the new standard. Frameworks will be written using DSLs, not on top of statically typed languages with restrictive syntax and unnecessary ceremony. Note that this isn't necessarily a dynamic language or even a Ruby tirade: a strong potential exists for statically typed type-inference languages that have a suitable syntax to also take advantage of this style of programming. For an example of this, check out Jaskell[*] and, in particular, the build DSL written on top of it called Neptune.[†] Neptune performs the same basic tasks as Ant, but it is written as a domain-specific language atop Jaskell. It shows how readable and concise you can make code in Jaskell, using a familiar problem domain.

> **NOTE**
> Dietzler's Law: even general-purpose programming languages suffer from the "80-10-10" rule.

The Law of Demeter

The *Law of Demeter* was developed at Northwestern University in the late '80s. It is best summarized by the phrase, "Only talk to your closest friends." The idea is that any given object shouldn't know anything about the internal details of the objects with which it interacts. The name of the law comes from the Roman goddess Demeter, the goddess of agriculture (and therefore of food distribution). Although she was not technically an ancient philosopher, her name makes her sound like one!

More formally, the Law of Demeter says that for any object and method, the only methods that should be invoked are the following:

- The methods of the object itself
- Parameters of the method
- Any objects created within the method

[*] Download at *http://jaskell.codehaus.org/*.

[†] Download at *http://jaskell.codehaus.org/Neptune*.

In most modern languages, you can make this even shorter using the heuristic "never use more than one dot for any method call." Here's an example.

Let's say you have a Person class with two fields: a name and Job. Job also has two fields: title and salary. The Law of Demeter says that it is not acceptable to call through Job within Person to get to the position field, like this:

```
Job job = new Job("Safety Engineer", 50000.00);
Person homer = new Person("Homer", job);

homer.getJob().setPosition("Janitor");
```

So, to make this adhere to the Law of Demeter, you can create a method on Person to change the job, and then ask the Job class to perform the work for you:

```
public PersonDemo() {
    Job job = new Job("Safety Engineer", 50000.00);
    Person homer = new Person("Homer", job);
    homer.changeJobPositionTo("Janitor");
}

public void changeJobPositionTo(String newPosition) {
    job.changePositionTo(newPosition);
}
```

What benefit has this change created? First, notice that we're no longer calling the setPosition method on the Job class, we're using a more descriptive method named changePositionTo. This emphasizes the fact that nothing outside the Job class has any idea of how position is implemented internally to Job. Although it looks like a String now, internally it might be an enumeration. This information-hiding is the main point: you don't want dependent objects knowing about implementation details of the internal workings of a class. The Law of Demeter prevents this by forcing you to write methods on classes that specifically hide those details.

When rigorously applied, you tend to end up with lots of small wrapper or proxy methods for your class that prevent multiple "dots" in method calls. What you buy with that extra code is looser coupling between classes, ensuring that changes to one class won't cause changes to another class. For a more elaborate example of the Law of Demeter, check out (part of the lore of software) "The Paperboy, The Wallet, and The Law Of Demeter" by David Bock.‡

Software Lore

Software developers are mostly ignorant of software lore. Because technology moves so quickly, developers have to struggle to keep up with all the changes. What could some ancient (relatively, that is) technology tell me about the kinds of problems I need to solve right now?

---

‡ Download at *http://www.ccs.neu.edu/research/demeter/demeter-method/LawOfDemeter/paper-boy/demeter.pdf.*

Certainly reading a book about the syntax of Smalltalk isn't going to help you if you write only in Java or C#. But all Smalltalk books don't have just syntax in them: they have the hard-won lessons of the developers who were using a brand-new technology (object-oriented languages) for the first time.

NOTE
Pay attention to the lore of "ancient" technologies.

Ancient philosophers created ideas that seem obvious in hindsight but that required great leaps of intellect and courage at the time. Sometimes they suffered greatly because what they said went against the established doctrines. One of the great rebels of history was Galileo, who apparently didn't believe anything that anyone told him. He always had to try it for himself. The accepted wisdom before his time maintained that a heavier object would fall faster than a lighter one. This was based on Aristotelian thinking, where thinking hard about something logically had more merit than experimenting. Galileo didn't buy it, so he went to the top of the Leaning Tower of Pisa and dropped rocks. And fired rocks from cannons. And discovered that, nonintuitively, all objects fall at the same rate (if you discount air resistance).

What Galileo did was prove that things that seem nonintuitive can in fact be true, which is still a valuable lesson. Some hard-fought knowledge about software development is not intuitive. The idea that you can design the entire software up front, and then just transcribe it seems logical, but it doesn't work in the real world of constant change. Fortunately, a giant catalog of nonintuitive software lore exists in the Anti Patterns catalog (*http://c2.com/cgi/wiki? AntiPatternsCatalog*). This is the ancient lore of software. Rather than gnashing your teeth in frustration when your boss is forcing you to use a library of subquality code, point out to him that he's falling into the "Standing on the Shoulder of Midgets" anti pattern, and he'll see that you aren't the only one who thinks it's a bad idea.

Understanding the existing software lore provides great resources when you are being asked to do something that you know in your gut is the wrong thing to do, and yet some manager-type is forcing the issue. Having an understanding of the battles fought in the past will give you the ammunition for your current battles. Take some time and read those decades-old software books that are still widely read, like *The Mythical Man-Month*, Hunt and Thomas's *The Pragmatic Programmer* (Addison-Wesley), and Beck's *Smalltalk Best Practice Patterns* (Prentice Hall). This isn't an exhaustive list by any means, but they all provide invaluable lore.

CHAPTER ELEVEN

Question Authority

GENERAL STANDARDIZATION ACROSS DEVELOPMENT TEAMS AND DEVELOPMENT COMMUNITIES is a good thing. It allows people to read each other's code more easily, understand idioms more readily, and avoid wildly idiomatic coding (except perhaps in the Perl community*).

But blind adherence to standards is just as bad as having no standards at all. Sometimes standards prevent useful deviations. For each of the things you do when developing software, make sure you know the reason *why* you are doing it. Otherwise, you may be suffering because of angry monkeys.

Angry Monkeys

This is a story I first heard from Dave Thomas during a keynote address he delivered called *Angry Monkeys and Cargo Cults*. I don't know if it's true (despite researching it quite a bit), but it doesn't matter—it illustrates a point beautifully.

Back in the 1960s (when scientists were allowed to do all kinds of crazy things), behavioral scientists conducted an experiment where they placed five monkeys in a room with a stepladder and a bunch of bananas hanging from the ceiling. The monkeys quickly figured out that they could climb the ladder and eat the bananas, but every time the monkeys got near the stepladder, the scientists would douse the entire room in ice cold water. You can guess what that generated: angry monkeys. Soon, none of the monkeys would go near the ladder.

Then, the scientists replaced one of the monkeys with a new monkey, who had not been subject to the blasts of water. The first thing he did was make a beeline for the ladder, and all the other monkeys beat him up. He didn't know *why* they were beating him up, but he quickly learned: don't go near the ladder. Gradually, the scientists replaced the original monkeys with new monkeys until they had a group of monkeys who had never been doused with cold water, yet they would still attack any monkey that approached the ladder.

The point? In software, lots of the practices on projects exist because "that's the way we've always done it." In other words, because of angry monkeys.

Here's an example that arose during one of my projects. Everyone knows that in Java method names are supposed to start with a lowercase letter, then use CamelCase, where word boundaries are indicated by a capital letter. That's fine for regular coding, but test names are different. When naming unit tests, you want a nice, long, descriptive name so that you can tell what's being tested. Unfortunately, `LongCamelCaseNamesAreHardToRead`. On this particular project, I suggested that we use underscores, between the words in test names, like this:

---

* I'm just kidding. Really. I love you guys! Please don't send me emails!

```
public void testUpdateCacheAndVerifyItemExists() {

}

public void test_Update_cache_and_verify_item_exists() {

}
```

To me, the underscored name was far more readable. It was interesting to watch the development team's reactions to my proposal. Some of the developers liked the idea immediately, and others looked like angry monkeys at my mere suggestion. We ended up using this style (tech leads get to be benevolent dictators sometimes) and found that it produced much more readable test names, especially when reading a long list of names in a test runner viewer of an IDE (see Figure 11-1).

"Because we've always done it this way" is not a sufficient reason for any development habit. If you *understand* why you have always done it that way, and it makes sense, then by all means continue. But you should always question assumptions and verify their validity.

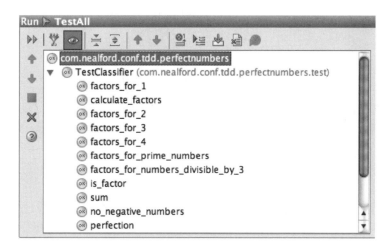

FIGURE 11-1. Underscored test names are more readable

Fluent Interfaces

A *fluent interface* is one of the types of domain-specific language (DSL) styles currently in vogue. In a fluent interface, you try to construct long sequences of code into sentences, rationalizing that complete chunks of thought in spoken languages follow this style. This style of coding is easier to read because, just like with English sentences, you know where one thought ends and the next begins.

Here is an example, based on one of my projects. We built an application that dealt with train cars, and each train car had a marketing description. Train cars have lots of rules and regulations associated with them, so getting testing scenarios just right was difficult. We constantly had to ask our business analysts if we had the perfectly nuanced definition of the type of car we needed to test. Here's a simplified version of what we showed them:

```
Car car = new CarImpl();
MarketingDescription desc = new MarketingDescriptionImpl();
desc.setType("Box");
desc.setSubType("Insulated");
desc.setAttribute("length", "50.5");
desc.setAttribute("ladder", "yes");
desc.setAttribute("lining type", "cork");
car.setDescription(desc);
```

While this looks perfectly normal to a Java developer, our business analysts hated it. "Why are you showing me Java code? Just tell me what you mean." Of course, translation always introduces the chance of error. To mitigate this problem, we created a fluent interface, capturing the same information, but in this form instead:

```
Car car = Car.describedAs()
              .box()
              .length(50.5)
              .type(Type.INSULATED)
              .includes(Equipment.LADDER)
              .lining(Lining.CORK);
```

Our business analysts liked this much better. We managed to get rid of much of the objectionable redundancy required in the "normal" Java API style. The implementation was very simple. All the set properties returned this instead of void, allowing us to create sentences by chaining the method calls together. The implementation of Car looked like the following:

```
public class Car {
    private MarketingDescription _desc;

    public Car() {
        _desc = new MarketingDescriptionImpl();
    }

    public static Car describedAs() {
        return new Car();
    }

    public Car box() {
        _desc.setType("box");
        return this;
    }

    public Car length(double length) {
        _desc.setLength(length);
        return this;
    }

    public Car type(Type type) {
        _desc.setType(type);
        return this;
    }
}
```

```
    public Car includes(Equipment equip) {
        _desc.setAttribute("equipment", equip.toString());
        return this;
    }

    public Car lining(Lining lining) {
        _desc.setLining(lining);
        return this;
    }
}
```

This is also an example of the DSL pattern known as an *expression builder*. The Car class hides the fact that it is actually building a MarketingDescription object internally. Expression builders make published interfaces over encapsulated expressions to simplify the fluent interface. To make the method-chaining possible, each of the mutator methods of Car returns this.

So why put this example in a chapter about questioning authority? To write a fluent interface like Car requires that you kill one of the sacred cows of Java: the Car class is no longer a JavaBean. While that doesn't seem like a big deal, much of the infrastructure of Java insists on this specification. But when you look closely at the JavaBeans specification, it does several things to harm the overall quality of your code.

The JavaBeans specification insists that every object have a default constructor (see "Constructors" in Chapter 8), yet virtually no object is valid if it has no state. The JavaBeans specification also mandates the ugly property syntax in Java, requiring getXXX() methods for accessors and setXXX() methods for mutators, which require a void return type. I understand why these limitations exist (for example, the default constructor makes it easier to handle serialization), but no one in the Java world questions whether they should make their objects beans. The default is to follow the other angry monkeys and make everything a bean.

Question authority. Making everything a bean makes it impossible to create a fluent interface. Know what you are creating, understand what it will be used for, and make decisions wisely. "Because that's the way everyone says it should be" is rarely the correct answer.

Anti-Objects

Sometimes the authority you should question is your own inclination toward a particular solution to a problem. A great paper appeared at the 2006 OOPSLA conference called "Collaborative Diffusion: Programming Anti-Objects."[†] The paper's authors make the point that, while objects and object hierarchies provide excellent abstraction mechanisms for most problems, those same abstractions make some problems more complex. The idea behind anti-objects is to switch the perceived foreground and background of the problem, and solve the simpler, less obvious problem. What is meant by "foreground" and "background"? An example will clarify. (Warning! If you still enjoy playing *PacMan*, don't read the next paragraphs—they will ruin it forever for you! Sometimes knowledge comes with a price.)

[†] Download at *http://www.cs.colorado.edu/~ralex/papers/PDF/OOPSLA06antiobjects.pdf*.

Consider the *PacMan* console game. When it came out in the 1970s, it had less computational ability than a cheap cell phone of today. Yet, it had to solve a really difficult math problem: how do you get the ghosts to chase PacMan through the maze? That is to say: what is the shortest distance to a moving target through a maze? That's a big problem, especially if you have very little memory or processor power to work with. So the developers of *PacMan* didn't solve that problem, they used the anti-object approach and built the intelligence into the maze itself.

The maze in *PacMan* acts like an automata (like in Conway's *Game of Life*). Each cell has simple rules associated with it, and the cells executed one at a time, starting at the upper left and proceeding to the lower right. Each cell remembers a value of "PacMan smell." When PacMan sits on a cell, it has maximum PacMan smell. If he had just vacated the cell, it has maximum PacMan smell –1. The smell degrades for a few more turns, then disappears. The ghosts can then be dumb: they just sniff for PacMan smell, and any time they encounter it, they go to the cell that has a stronger smell.

The "obvious" solution to the problem builds intelligence into the ghosts. Yet, the much simpler solution builds the intelligence into the maze. That is the anti-object approach: flip the computational foreground and background. Don't fall into the trap of thinking that "traditional" modeling is always the correct solution. Perhaps a particular problem is more easily solved in another language entirely. (See Chapter 14 for the rationale behind this anti-object approach.)

CHAPTER TWELVE

Meta-Programming

META-PROGRAMMING IS FORMALLY DEFINED AS WRITING PROGRAMS THAT WRITE PROGRAMS, but the practical definition is much broader. In general, any solution that manipulates code outside "normal" use is considered meta-programming. Meta-programming approaches tend to be more complex than traditional solutions (for example, libraries and frameworks), but because you are manipulating code at a more fundamental level, it makes hard things easier and impossible things merely improbable.

All major modern languages have some level of meta-programming support. Learning the meta-programming facilities of your primary language will save you major effort and open new avenues to finding solutions.

I talk about several examples of meta-programming in this chapter, giving you a flavor in Java, Groovy, and Ruby. Each language's capabilities are different; the following examples simply show the kinds of problems you can solve using meta-programming.

Java and Reflection

Java's reflection is robust but limited. You can certainly call methods with String representations of their names, but the security manager won't allow you to define new methods or overwrite existing methods at runtime. You can do some of that with Aspects, but that's arguably not really Java because it has its own syntax, compiler, etc.

An example of when you might want to use Java's reflection is for testing private methods. When you are writing code using test-driven development (TDD), you still want to use the protection mechanisms built-in to the language. Using reflection to call the private method is pretty straightforward, but requires lots of syntax.

Let's say that you needed to call a method named isFactor (which returns whether a number is a factor of another number) on a class named Classifier. To call the private isFactor method, you can create a helper method in your test class that looks like this:

```
private boolean isFactor(int factor, int number) {
    Method m;
    try {
        m = Classifier.class.getDeclaredMethod("isFactor",
                int.class);
        m.setAccessible(true);❶
        return (Boolean) m.invoke(new Classifier(number), factor);❷
    } catch (Throwable t) {
        fail();❸
    }
    return false;
}
```

❶ The call to setAccessible changes the scoping of the method to public.

❷ The invoke method makes the actual call, with the requisite type casing of the return value (which, in this case, is autoboxed back to a primitive boolean).

❸ Regardless of the exception thrown, the unit test fails because something went wrong.

The unit test then becomes trivial:

```
@Test public void is_factor() {
    assertTrue(isFactor(1, 10));
    assertTrue(isFactor(5, 25));
    assertFalse(isFactor(6, 25));
}
```

In the previous example, you just ate whatever exceptions occurred because of the reflection code (Java is very worried about reflection and requires that you catch a lot of different types of exceptions). Most of the time you can get by with failing the test because something's just not working. In other situations, though, you have to be a little more careful. Here's an example of a test class helper that has to tiptoe around the exceptions that legitimately bubble out of the method called via reflection:

```
private void calculateFactors(Classifier c) {
    Method m;
    try {
        m = Classifier.class.getDeclaredMethod("calculateFactors");
        m.setAccessible(true);
        m.invoke(c);
    } catch (InvocationTargetException t) {
        if (t.getTargetException() instanceof InvalidNumberException)
            throw (InvalidNumberException) t.getTargetException();
        else
            fail();
    } catch (Throwable e) {
        fail();
    }
}
```

In this case, you look to see if you care about the exception and, if so, rethrow it and swallow everything else.

The ability to call methods via reflection makes it possible to build much more intelligent factory classes, allowing the loading of classes at runtime. Most plug-in architectures use the ability to load classes and call methods via reflection to allow people to build new stuff that adheres to a particular interface without having to have the concrete classes around at compile time.

The reflection (and other meta-programming) facilities in Java are weak compared to those in dynamic languages. C# has slightly better, more extensive meta-programming support, but it is in the same general ballpark as Java.

Testing Java with Groovy

Groovy is the dynamic language syntax for Java. As such, it can interact pretty seamlessly with Java code (including compiled byte code), allowing you much more flexible syntax. Groovy makes it possible for you to do a bunch of stuff on the Java platform that is difficult or impossible using Java.

You can invoke the standard reflection mechanism in Java using the Groovy syntax as shown in this listing, which replicates the test for isFactor shown earlier:

```
@Test public void is_factor_via_reflection() {
  def m = Classifier.class.getDeclaredMethod("isFactor", int.class)
  m.accessible = true
  assertTrue m.invoke(new Classifier(10), 10)
  assertTrue m.invoke(new Classifier(25), 5)
  assertFalse m.invoke(new Classifier(25), 6)
}
```

As you can see, the reflection code is so concise that I didn't feel compelled to put it in its own method. Groovy swallows the noisy checked exceptions for you, making it easier (or at least less formal) to call the reflection methods. Groovy "understands" Java property syntax so that the call m.accessible = true is equivalent to the call Java m.setAccessible(true). Groovy also has looser rules about parentheses.

The code shown here tests the exact same code as the unit test shown above—it literally uses the same JAR file to access the code. Groovy makes it easier to write unit tests for Java code, which is a good excuse for "sneaking" it into conservative organizations (after all, testing code is part of the infrastructure, not deployed to production, so who cares what open source libraries you use, right?). In fact, I'm a big advocate of not calling "Groovy" by its name when nondevelopers are around. I prefer calling it the Enterprise Business Execution Language (using the acronym ebXl—managers think that acronyms with capital *X*s in them are sexy).

Actually, the earlier test isn't the entire story. It turns out that in its current incarnation, Groovy ignores the private keyword entirely, even when something is declared private in Java code. Thus, the earlier test could be written like this:

```
@Test public void is_factor() {
    assertTrue new Classifier(10).isFactor(1)
    assertTrue new Classifier(25).isFactor(5)
    assertFalse new Classifier(25).isFactor(6)
}
```

Yes, this is calling the Java code from the JAR file, where the isFactor method is private. Groovy conveniently ignores privates, so you can just call the methods directly. Groovy is using reflection underneath to call the methods anyway, so it is just silently calling the setAccessible method for you. Technically, this is a bug in Groovy (that has been there since day one), but it's so insanely useful, no one has bothered to fix it. And I hope they never do. In any language with strong reflection capabilities, the private keyword is not much more than documentation anyway: I can always use reflection to get to it if the need arises.

Writing Fluent Interfaces

Here is a short example of using Ruby's meta-programming support to write a fluent interface that goes beyond Java's capabilities. Obviously, an entire book could be written about this subject—this will just give you a taste. This code works on any version of Ruby, including the Java platform port, JRuby.

You want to write a fluent interface that represents recipes. It should allow developers to write the ingredients for the recipes in what looks like a data format, but underneath it should build a nutrition profile. The ability to encapsulate the actual behavior of code is one of the advantages of fluent interfaces. Here is the target syntax:

```
recipe = Recipe.new "Spicy bread"
recipe.add 200.grams.of Flour
recipe.add 1.lb.of Nutmeg
```

To make this code work, you must first add new methods to the built-in Numeric class in Ruby (which encompasses both integer and floating-point numbers):

```
class Numeric❶
  def gram
    self
  end
  alias_method :grams, :gram❷

  def pound
    self * 453.59237
  end
  alias_method :pounds, :pound
  alias_method :lb, :pound
  alias_method :lbs, :pound
end
```

❶ The Numeric class is already on the classpath, so this reopens the class to allow adding new methods.

❷ alias_method is a built-in Ruby facility to allow you to create aliases (in other words, friendly names) for existing methods. alias_method isn't a keyword; it is part of the meta-programming built-in to Ruby.

Open classes in Ruby allow you to add new methods to existing classes. The syntax is quite simple: when you create a class definition, it opens the existing class if that class already appears on the classpath. The built-in Numeric type is obviously already on the classpath, so this code adds new methods to it. I'm keeping track of recipe weights in grams, so the gram method merely returns the value of the number, and pound returns the number of grams in a pound.

The changes to the Numeric class make the first part of my recipe fluent interface work. What about the second part?

```
class Numeric
  def of ingredient
    if ingredient.kind_of? String
      ingredient = Ingredient.new(ingredient)
    end
    ingredient.quantity = self
    return ingredient
  end
end
```

Reopening Numeric again allows you to add the of method to numbers. This method works with either Strings or existing ingredients (the code checks to see what has been passed), sets the quantity of the Ingredient object to the value of the number, and then returns the ingredient instance (the return isn't strictly necessary; the last line of any Ruby method is the return of the method, but the explicit call makes the code a little more readable).

This unit test verifies that all these changes work correctly:

```ruby
def test_full_recipe
  recipe = Recipe.new
  expected = [] << 2.lbs.of("Flour") << 1.gram.of("Nutmeg")
  expected.each {|i| recipe.add i}
  assert_equal 2, recipe.ingredients.size
  assert_equal("Flour", recipe.ingredients[0].name)
  assert_equal(2 * 453.59237, recipe.ingredients[0].quantity)
  assert_equal("Nutmeg", recipe.ingredients[1].name)
  assert_equal(1, recipe.ingredients[1].quantity)
end
```

Building fluent interfaces is much easier in dynamic languages because they allow you facilities like open classes and literal numbers as objects. Adding methods via open classes may seem an odd way to solve a problem to Java and C# developers, but it is a natural way to build code in Ruby and Groovy.

> **NOTE**
> Meta-programming changes your syntactic vocabulary, giving you more ways to express yourself.

Whither Meta-Programming?

Seeing all this meta-programming code may make you queasy because it violates the cardinal rule of not writing self-modifying code. But this is precisely a place where you should question authority (see Chapter 11). Yes, this can be dangerous, *when used incorrectly.* But that's true of any powerful feature. You can do dangerous things using Aspects in Java as well, it's just more difficult. But it's a bad argument to say that powerful language features should be so difficult that only masters can attain them. Much of the philosophy of Java was to remove power from the hands of developers by making the String class final. But an interesting thing happened: building restrictions into the language didn't make the poor developers any better, and it placed a governor on the best developers, making them jump through ridiculous hoops to get things done. The classic example playing out right now in Groovy concerns how to handle GStrings. The GString is the String class in Groovy that offers lots more features than the Java String. Because Groovy interacts so intimately with Java, it would be helpful to be able to use String and GString interchangeably, certainly in Groovy code that passes strings to Java code. But you can't. Because the String class is declared as final, you can't even subclass GStrings from Strings so that Java libraries can understand them. The existence of final is an admission of the language designers that they don't trust the people using the language.

Languages with strong meta-programming support take the opposite approach: they allow developers extraordinary power, and let them decide when to use it.

CHAPTER THIRTEEN

Composed Method and SLAP

SLAP STANDS FOR THE SINGLE LEVEL OF ABSTRACTION PRINCIPLE. While the concept comes from Kent Beck's *Smalltalk Best Practice Patterns* (Prentice Hall), my friend Glenn Vanderburg is the one who captured its essence with this great acronym.

Before I talk about SLAP, though, I must talk about the *composed method* pattern discussed in Beck's book. Composed method mandates that all public methods read like an outline of the steps to perform. The actual steps are implemented as private methods. Composed method is a way of factoring your code to keep it cohesive and make it easier to spot candidates for code reuse. The best way to understand composed method is to see it in action.

Composed Method in Action

Composed method encourages factoring (or refactoring) code into small, cohesive, readable chunks. For projects on which I'm the tech lead, our rule of thumb is to allow no method to exceed 15 lines of code in Java or C#. For dynamic languages such as Groovy or Ruby, the rule is five lines of code.

What benefit does this provide? Consider the following noncomposed method code, from a small e-commerce site:

```
public void populate() throws Exception  {
    Connection c = null;
    try {
        Class.forName(DRIVER_CLASS);
        c = DriverManager.getConnection(DB_URL, USER, PASSWORD);
        Statement stmt = c.createStatement();
        ResultSet rs = stmt.executeQuery(SQL_SELECT_PARTS);
        while (rs.next()) {
            Part p = new Part();
            p.setName(rs.getString("name"));
            p.setBrand(rs.getString("brand"));
            p.setRetailPrice(rs.getDouble("retail_price"));
            partList.add(p);
        }
    } finally {
        c.close();
    }
}
```

This method is part of a larger class that uses low-level Java Database Connectivity (JDBC) to harvest information from a database. Nothing in this code really jumps out as a candidate for reuse. But it violates the 15-line guideline, and it seems like it's doing a lot of stuff, so you should refactor it.

The first step entails refactoring out the parts that seem like the steps you're performing. If you wrote out in English what this method does, you'd have a good idea what the new method names should be. After a refactoring pass, you end up with this:

```
public class PartDb {
    private static final String DRIVER_CLASS =
            "com.mysql.jdbc.Driver";
    private static final String DB_URL =
            "jdbc:mysql://localhost/orderentry";
```

```
private static final int DEFAULT_INITIAL_LIST_SIZE = 40;
private static final String SQL_SELECT_PARTS =
        "select name, brand, retail_price from parts";
private static final Part[] TEMPLATE = new Part[0];
private ArrayList partList;

public PartDb() {
    partList = new ArrayList(DEFAULT_INITIAL_LIST_SIZE);
}

public Part[] getParts() {
    return (Part[]) partList.toArray(TEMPLATE);
}

public void populate() throws Exception {
    Connection c = null;
    try {
        c = getDatabaseConnection();
        ResultSet rs = createResultSet(c);
        while (rs.next())
            addPartToListFromResultSet(rs);
    } finally {
        c.close();
    }
}

private ResultSet createResultSet(Connection c)
        throws SQLException {
    return c.createStatement().
            executeQuery(SQL_SELECT_PARTS);
}

private Connection getDatabaseConnection()
        throws ClassNotFoundException, SQLException {
    Connection c;
    Class.forName(DRIVER_CLASS);
    c = DriverManager.getConnection(DB_URL,
            "webuser", "webpass");
    return c;
}

private void addPartToListFromResultSet(ResultSet rs)
        throws SQLException {
    Part p = new Part();
    p.setName(rs.getString("name"));
    p.setBrand(rs.getString("brand"));
    p.setRetailPrice(rs.getDouble("retail_price"));
    partList.add(p);
}
}
```

OK, this is better. You can see that the populate method now reads like an outline of the steps required:

1. Get the database connection.

2. Create the result set from the connection.

3. For each of the items in the result set, add the items to the Part list.

4. Close the database connection.

The populate method now adheres to the composed method guideline, but notice what else has happened. The getDatabaseConnection method has nothing to do with Parts: it is just generic code to get a database connection. You can push it up the inheritance hierarchy and reuse it for other database classes. Similarly, the only thing tying the createResultSet method to Parts is the SQL string. We can make that generic too. Acting on these two improvements, you end up with two classes—BoundaryBase and PartDb:

```
abstract public class BoundaryBase {
    private static final String DRIVER_CLASS =
            "com.mysql.jdbc.Driver";
    private static final String DB_URL =
            "jdbc:mysql://localhost/orderentry";

    protected Connection getDatabaseConnection() throws ClassNotFoundException,
            SQLException {
        Connection c;
        Class.forName(DRIVER_CLASS);
        c = DriverManager.getConnection(DB_URL, "webuser", "webpass");
        return c;
    }
    // . . .
```

The BoundaryBase class now has the getDatabaseConnection method, and the two constants it used came along with it.

To refactor the createResultSet method, take advantage of the *template method design pattern,* from the classic Gang of Four book, Gamma et al.'s *Design: Elements of Reusable Object-Oriented Software Patterns* (Addison-Wesley). Template method states that you should create abstract methods in the parent class, deferring implementation details to methods in the child class. This pattern is a way to define common algorithmic structure, supplying details for later. To that end, you refactor the createResultSet method up into BoundaryBase, along with an abstract method placeholder to force the child class to supply the SQL string. In this example, you refactor the createResultSet method into two methods, one retaining the original name, and a new abstract method that the child uses to supply the SQL string (getSqlForEntity):

```
abstract protected String getSqlForEntity();

protected ResultSet createResultSet(Connection c) throws SQLException {
    Statement stmt = c.createStatement();
    return stmt.executeQuery(getSqlForEntity());
}
```

OK, that was fun. Let's see if any more of the code in the original populate method is abstractable. If you look at the populate method itself, the only thing tying it to this particular entity is the body of the while loop, which takes the items from the result set and populates the entities. You can use the same template method trick here and drag the entire populate method up to the BoundaryBase class:

```
abstract protected void addEntityToListFromResultSet(ResultSet rs)
        throws SQLException;

public void populate() throws Exception {
    Connection c = null;
    try {
```

```
        c = getDatabaseConnection();
        ResultSet rs = createResultSet(c);
        while (rs.next())
            addEntityToListFromResultSet(rs);
    } finally {
        c.close();
    }
}
```

Just as before, the algorithm for pulling stuff from a result set and putting it into a list of entities is common across lots of domain entities, so why not make it more generic?

Now, have a look at the `PartDb` class after all the refactoring:

```java
public class PartDb extends BoundaryBase {
    private static final int DEFAULT_INITIAL_LIST_SIZE = 40;
    private static final String SQL_SELECT_PARTS =
            "select name, brand, retail_price from parts";
    private static final Part[] TEMPLATE = new Part[0];
    private ArrayList partList;

    public PartDb() {
        partList = new ArrayList(DEFAULT_INITIAL_LIST_SIZE);
    }

    public Part[] getParts() {
        return (Part[]) partList.toArray(TEMPLATE);
    }

    protected String getSqlForEntity() {
        return SQL_SELECT_PARTS;
    }

    protected void addEntityToListFromResultSet(ResultSet rs) throws SQLException {
        Part p = new Part();
        p.setName(rs.getString("name"));
        p.setBrand(rs.getString("brand"));
        p.setRetailPrice(rs.getDouble("retail_price"));
        partList.add(p);
    }
}
```

The only things left in this class pertain directly to the `Part` entity. All the rest of the code that handles the mechanics of populating the entity from a result set now resides in the `BoundaryBase` class, ready to be reused for other entites.

Three things pop out of this example. First, notice how the first version of the code didn't seem like it contained any reusable code. It was just a lump of code that did some uninteresting stuff. Once you applied composed method, though, reusable assets fell out of it. Noncohesive methods make it hard to see any reusable code that you might have. Forcing yourself to break it up into atomic pieces reveals reusable code you might never have realized you had.

NOTE
Refactoring to composed method reveals hidden reusable code.

Second, you now have a clean partition between the boilerplate mechanical code to get stuff from a database and the actual details needed for a particular entity. That means that you have the beginnings of a simple persistence framework. The `BoundaryBase` class is the start of an *extracted* framework to handle persistence. Remember back in Chapter 9: the best frameworks are those extracted from working code. This example contains the seeds of a simple persistence framework.

Third, composed method exposes places where you have repeated code without realizing it (see Chapter 5). Repetition is insidious; it pops up everywhere in software development, even in places where you would swear that you hadn't repeated anything.

One other thing about composed method: if you are rigorous about test-driven development TDD (see Chapter 6), you pretty much automatically get composed method code. TDD encourages, actually forces, you to write really cohesive methods (the smallest thing for which you can write a test), which lends itself to composed method.

> **NOTE**
> TDD predisposes composed method.

SLAP

SLAP insists that all your code within a method live at the same level of abstraction. In other words, you shouldn't have a method in which part of it deals with low-level database connectivity, another part with high-level business code, and another with web service plumbing. Of course, such a method would also violate Beck's composed method rule. But even if you have a cohesive method, you should make sure that all the lines of code share the same abstraction level.

Here's an example. Consider this method, taken from a sample JEE e-commerce site (slightly more complex than the one in the previous examples). This particular method takes a shopping cart and adds an order (which in turn adds line items). For simplicity's sake, it also uses low-level JDBC, but that's peripheral to the SLAP discussion.

```
public void addOrder(ShoppingCart cart, String userName,
                     Order order) throws SQLException {
    Connection c = null;
    PreparedStatement ps = null;
    Statement s = null;
    ResultSet rs = null;
    boolean transactionState = false;
    try {
        c = dbPool.getConnection();
        s = c.createStatement();
        transactionState = c.getAutoCommit();
        int userKey = getUserKey(userName, c, ps, rs);
        c.setAutoCommit(false);
        addSingleOrder(order, c, ps, userKey);❶
        int orderKey = getOrderKey(s, rs);
        addLineItems(cart, c, orderKey);
        c.commit();
```

```
            order.setOrderKeyFrom(orderKey);
        } catch (SQLException sqlx) {
            s = c.createStatement();
            c.rollback();
            throw sqlx;
        } finally {
            try {
                c.setAutoCommit(transactionState);
                dbPool.release(c);
                if (s != null)
                    s.close();
                if (ps != null)
                    ps.close();
                if (rs != null)
                    rs.close();
            } catch (SQLException ignored) {
            }
        }
    }
```

❶ This method is at a different level of abstraction than the ones preceding it.

The addOrder method consists of a bunch of steps to set up database infrastructure, then moves to higher-level business domain methods like addSingleOrder. It is hard to read code like this because it leaps between abstraction levels almost randomly, based on what steps need to occur next.

One pass at refactoring later, keeping composed method in mind, yields a cleaner version of the same method:

```
public void addOrder(ShoppingCart cart, String userName,
                     Order order) throws SQLException {
    Connection connection = null;
    PreparedStatement ps = null;
    Statement statement = null;
    ResultSet rs = null;
    boolean transactionState = false;
    try {
        connection = dbPool.getConnection();
        statement = connection.createStatement();
        transactionState =
                setupTransactionStateFor(connection,
                        transactionState);
        addSingleOrder(order, connection,
                ps, userKeyFor(userName, connection));
        order.setOrderKeyFrom(generateOrderKey(statement, rs));
        addLineItems(cart, connection, order.getOrderKey());
        completeTransaction(connection);
    } catch (SQLException sqlx) {
        rollbackTransactionFor(connection);
        throw sqlx;
    } finally {
        cleanUpDatabaseResources(connection,
                transactionState, statement, ps, rs);
    }
}


private void cleanUpDatabaseResources(Connection connection,
        boolean transactionState, Statement s,
        PreparedStatement ps, ResultSet rs) throws SQLException {
```

```
        connection.setAutoCommit(transactionState);
        dbPool.release(connection);
        if (s != null)
            s.close();
        if (ps != null)
            ps.close();
        if (rs != null)
            rs.close();
    }

    private void rollbackTransactionFor(Connection connection)❶
            throws SQLException {
        connection.rollback();
    }

    private void completeTransaction(Connection c)
            throws SQLException {
        c.commit();
    }

    private boolean setupTransactionStateFor(Connection c,
            boolean transactionState) throws SQLException {
        transactionState = c.getAutoCommit();
        c.setAutoCommit(false);
        return transactionState;
    }
```

❶ It's OK to have single-line methods if it improves the abstraction level of the code around it.

This code covers many more methods (including a couple of single-line methods), but it does a much better job of not jumping abstraction levels unnecessarily. Of course, Java requires a bit of cruft up front to handle all the initializations, and the whole method body must reside inside a try...catch block to handle database rollback if any errors occur. The addOrder method reads much better now. This embodies the ideal of composed method: the body of the public method reads like an outline of the steps required, with a few distractions imposed by Java thrown in.

Can you clean up this code any more? It still has a fair amount of low-level noise required by Java. This listing incrementally improves upon the previous one by storing all the plumbing objects in a Map and writing methods to accept all the JDBC parts from the Map instead of individually:

```
public void addOrderFrom(ShoppingCart cart, String userName,
                Order order) throws SQLException {
    Map db = setupDataInfrastructure();
    try {
        int userKey = userKeyBasedOn(userName, db);
        add(order, userKey, db);
        addLineItemsFrom(cart,
                order.getOrderKey(), db);
        completeTransaction(db);
    } catch (SQLException sqlx) {
        rollbackTransactionFor(db);
        throw sqlx;
    } finally {
        cleanUp(db);
    }
}
```

```
private Map setupDataInfrastructure() throws SQLException {
    HashMap db = new HashMap();
    Connection c = dbPool.getConnection();
    db.put("connection", c);
    db.put("transaction state",
            Boolean.valueOf(setupTransactionStateFor(c)));
    return db;
}

private void cleanUp(Map db) throws SQLException {
    Connection connection = (Connection) db.get("connection");
    boolean transactionState = ((Boolean)
            db.get("transation state")).booleanValue();
    Statement s = (Statement) db.get("statement");
    PreparedStatement ps = (PreparedStatement)
            db.get("prepared statement");
    ResultSet rs = (ResultSet) db.get("result set");
    connection.setAutoCommit(transactionState);
    dbPool.release(connection);
    if (s != null)
        s.close();
    if (ps != null)
        ps.close();
    if (rs != null)
        rs.close();
}

private void rollbackTransactionFor(Map dbInfrastructure)
        throws SQLException {
    ((Connection) dbInfrastructure.get("connection")).rollback();
}

private void completeTransaction(Map dbInfrastructure)
        throws SQLException {
    ((Connection) dbInfrastructure.get("connection")).commit();
}

private boolean setupTransactionStateFor(Connection c)
        throws SQLException {
    boolean transactionState = c.getAutoCommit();
    c.setAutoCommit(false);
    return transactionState;
}
```

This version sacrifices the readability of the helper methods for the readability of the public addOrderFrom method (renamed to make the calling more understandable). The biggest change is carrying all the logically but syntactically distinct database fields around in a Map, simplifying the method signatures. You'll also notice that I moved all the parameters for dbInfrastructure to the last parameter position, de-emphasizing the importance of the plumbing to the readability of the public addOrderFrom method.

Frequently, refactoring for clarity and readability has tradeoffs. A certain amount of essential complexity exists by default, so the question becomes "Where should complexity manifest itself?" I would rather have simpler public methods, and push complexity (in this example, in the form of packaging and unpackaging from the Map) into private methods. While implementing a class, you are already immersed in the details of the individual lines of code, so it is preferable to deal with complexity there. When reading public methods much later, you will prefer not to have to understand any nuance; you will just want to understand what the code does as simply as possible.

NOTE
Encapsulate all implementation details away from public methods.

Whether you prefer the second or third version of the code, both apply the SLAP principle: keep lines of code within a method at the same level of abstraction via aggressive refactoring.

CHAPTER FOURTEEN

Polyglot Programming

COMPUTER LANGUAGES, LIKE SHARKS, CAN'T SIT STILL OR THEY WILL DIE. Just like spoken languages, computer languages continuously evolve (although, fortunately, we don't have teenagers adding slang to our computer languages at the rate at which they are adding it to the English language). Languages evolve to meet the changing environments in which they find themselves. For example, Java recently added generics and annotations in its continuing arms race with .NET. At some point, though, this becomes counterproductive. If you look at a couple of languages from the past (Algol 68 or Ada), you will see that there is a limit to how far you can push a language before it becomes cumbersome and starts to collapse under its own weight. Have we reached that point with Java? And, if we have, what does the future hold?

This chapter introduces the idea of polyglot programming as the future of the Java and .NET platform and all those who love it and hold it dear. But, before we get into that, we need to see how we got to where we are now. What's wrong with Java, and how is this new idea going to fix it?

How Did We Get Here? And Where Exactly Is Here?

Java is an entrenched mainstay of corporate and other development today. It has been amazing to watch for those of us who lived in a time when Java was either an Indonesian island or a beverage. But popularity doesn't equate with perfection: Java has its share of warts, mostly due to legacy baggage (which is interesting, as Java was created as a new language and didn't have any backward compatibly requirements). Let's look at how Java got here, and just where "here" is.

Java's Birth and Upbringing

A mythical creature of the dim past (let's call him James) needed to build a new language for toasters and cable TV boxes. He didn't want to use the languages he already knew and loved (C and C++) because, even for someone who loved them, they were ill-suited to this type of job. Sure, you can reboot a computer a couple of times a day because of memory management problems, but it's extra-annoying to do that for a cable box.

One day, James decided to create a new language that would solve some of the problems of the beloved but flawed existing languages. He created Oak, which then became Java. (OK, I skipped a few parts of this legend.) And it was good. Java fixed many of the ills of C and C++, and hitched a ride on the burgeoning Internet. Bruce Tate called Java's rise in popularity a "perfect storm": all the right conditions fell into place to support Java's meteoric rise in popularity and use.

When Java first came out, the Internet and browsers were everyone's darlings. Java was a bit slow on that era's hardware and operating systems, but it could perform a trick that no one else could: run in a browser as an *applet*. While that seems odd now, applets were the thing that put Java on everyone's radar. Of course, ironically enough, things have come full circle: we're writing rich client applications that run in a browser, but now mostly with JavaScript, which is seeing its own resurgence in popularity.

By the time everyone figured out that running huge corporate applications in a browser wasn't a good idea, server-side Java had made its debut, adding words like *servlet* and *Tomcat* to everyone's vocabulary.

The Dark Side of Java

Just because Java came along at the right time and in the right place doesn't mean that it is a perfect solution. Java has some interesting baggage, all the more interesting considering that it didn't have to have *any* baggage, being a brand-new language. The baggage in Java consists of all those things that, when you were learning Java, you said to yourself, "You've got to be kidding—it works *how*?" You've probably forgotten most of those moments because that's Just the Way It Works. But let us revive some of those things for a bit.

That happens when?

Consider for a moment the order in which things get initialized in Java. Initialization is the job of the constructor, right? Well, right and wrong. Java allows you to create *static initializers* and *instance initializers* as well. Static initializers run before the constructor, and instance initializers run sometime around when the constructor runs. And you can have as many as you want. Oh, and you can call the constructors on objects as you declare them. Which comes first: the static initializer, the instance initializer, or the initialization of the declared (and constructed) object? Confused yet? Consider the following:

```
public class LoadEmUp {
    private Parent _parent = new Parent();

    { System.out.println("Told you so");
    }

    static {
        System.out.println("Did too");
    }

    public LoadEmUp() {
        System.out.println("Did not");
        _parent = new Parent(this);
    }

    static {
        System.out.println("Did not");
    }

    public static void main(String[] args) {
        new LoadEmUp();
        System.out.println("Did too");
        Parent referee = new Parent();
    }
}
```

```
class Parent {

    public Parent() {
        System.out.println("stop fighting!");
    }

    public Parent(Object owner) {
        System.out.println("I told you to stop fighting!");
    }
}
```

Without referring to documentation, can you predict the order in which the messages will appear? In case you aren't sure, here is the actual output of this application:

```
Did too
Did not
stop fighting!
Told you so
Did not
I told you to stop fighting!
Did too stop fighting!
```

Becoming part of the Java priesthood entails learning arcane, seemingly arbitrary facts like this.

Startup behavior is just the tip of the iceberg when it comes to strange little Java behaviors. Some bizarre things were encoded directly into the language, like array indexes.

Zero-based arrays make sense to...

...people who use languages that make heavy use of pointers. Did you ever ask yourself why arrays in Java are zero-based? It makes no sense. Of course, arrays in Java are zero-based because arrays in C are zero-based: backward compatibility with a language for which Java isn't backward compatible.

Zero-based arrays make perfect sense in C because an array in C is really just shorthand for pointer arithmetic. Consider the diagram in Figure 14-1. Arrays in C are essentially just syntactic sugar for manipulating pointers and offsets. (It could be argued that virtually everything in C is syntactic sugar for pointers, but that is a digression.)

```
int[] arr = malloc (sizeof(int), 2);
```

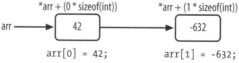

FIGURE 14-1. Array offsets in C

So, arrays in Java are zero-based because arrays in C are zero-based. While this makes sense in terms of programmer comfort level (i.e., making it easy to move from C/C++ to Java), it makes no sense from a language standpoint. Developers quickly lose old idioms when moving to new languages. If Java had included a foreach keyword from the outset, no one would have cared about the index number of arrays. Of course, Java finally did get a foreach operator (called, confusingly enough, for, just like the other one), and it took only eight years!

This fetish for zero-based arrays and slavish backward compatibility to C gave us the (original) for statement syntax as well:

```
for (int i = 0; i < 10; i++) {
    // some code
}
```

To C programmers, this is like going home again. To developers who have never seen or used C (an increasingly large number these days), it's just bizarre. Clearly, angry monkeys determined this syntax.

Java includes a depressingly large number of strange quirks and idioms, some anew from the Java creators, some existing as baggage from a previous life. All languages are like that, to varying degrees. Is there a way to escape this madness?

Where Are We Going? And How Do We Get There?

Fortunately, the creators of Java actually built two things: the Java language *and* the Java platform. And the latter is our escape hatch away from the baggage of the past. Increasingly, Java is being used more as a platform than a language. This trend is going to continue and pick up steam over the next couple of years. In fact, we will eventually all be engaged in what I call polyglot programming.

Polyglot Programming Today

When we build web applications today, we primarily develop in three languages (four, if you count XML): Java (or some other base, general-purpose language), SQL, and JavaScript (in the form of Ajax libraries). Yet most developers will say they are Java (or .NET or Ruby) programmers, leaving out the special-purpose languages that have infiltrated their "normal" general-purpose language.

Polyglot programming refers to building applications using one or more special-purpose languages in addition to a general-purpose language. We already do this, but it is so natural that we don't even think about it. For example, SQL has so ingrained itself into application development that it is taken for granted that virtually every application will use it.

SQL is a strange beast, though, compared to the general-purpose, imperative languages we generally use. SQL is all about set theory and manipulating data. As such, it doesn't look or feel like a "regular" language. Most developers are fine with this dichotomy. They happily use SQL (or allow Hibernate to generate it for them), debug bizarre SQL problems, and even help databases optimize SQL based on profiling. This is a mundanely natural part of everyday software development.

Today's Platform, Tomorrow's Languages

Why do we use special-purpose languages? Well, to serve special purposes. SQL clearly belongs in that category. JavaScript does as well, especially the way we use it today. Even though these different languages target different platforms (Java on the virtual machine, SQL on the database server, JavaScript in the browser), they all coalesce into an "application."

We should leverage this idea and make better use of it. The Java platform now supports a huge number of languages, some of them highly specialized for different tasks. This is our "get out of jail" card for the bizarreness of the Java language.

Groovy is an open source language that updates Java with dynamic language syntax and capabilities. It generates Java byte code, and therefore targets the Java platform. But Groovy's syntax is heavily influenced by the languages that have come along since Java's inception more than a decade ago. Groovy features closures, looser typing, collections that "understand" iteration, and a host of modern language improvements. And, it compiles down to good old Java byte code.

Here is an explicit example. As an experienced Java developer, your task is to write a simple program that reads a text file and prints out the contents of the text file with line numbers added to the front of each line. Think about writing that application for a second. It'll probably look something like this:

```java
public class LineNumbers {
    public LineNumbers(String path) {
        File file = new File(path);
        LineNumberReader reader = null;
        try {
            reader = new LineNumberReader(new FileReader(file));
            while (reader.ready()) {
                out.println(reader.getLineNumber() + ":"
                        + reader.readLine());
            }
        } catch (FileNotFoundException e) {
            e.printStackTrace();
        } catch (IOException e) {
            e.printStackTrace();
        } finally {
            try {
                reader.close();
            } catch (IOException ignored) {
            }
        }
    }

    public static void main(String[] args) {
        new LineNumbers(args[0]);
    }
}
```

Here is the complete Groovy application to do the same thing:

```
def number=0
new File (args[0]).eachLine { line ->
    number++
    println "$number: $line"
}
```

How many lines did that Java solution have? At some point, the syntactic requirements of Java become more of a constraint than an assistance. The Groovy version has fewer symbols than the Java one has lines of code! If Java and Groovy produce the same byte code, why use the fossilized Java syntax?

I can hear the hue and cry of Java developers everywhere: "The Groovy code won't be as efficient as the Java code!" And you are absolutely correct: Groovy adds overhead to Java byte code, inserting the required declarations, constructs, exception blocks, and other ritualized elements Java requires. The Java version will run hundreds of milliseconds faster than the Groovy version. Who cares? Developer productivity is more important than machine cycles, and Moore's law (which states the processor power doubles every 18 months) will see to it that this trend continues. Increasingly, we care more about getting work done with the fewest impediments than the raw performance characteristics of our code. Think back on the last five applications you wrote: in almost every case, wasn't the network and database latency a much bigger concern than the execution speed of the language?

Groovy is an obvious candidate to help modernize the crusty bits of the Java language. Yet this idea of polyglot programming will go much deeper than just putting a Groovy facade over our byte code. Increasingly, we'll leverage this idea to enable kinds of applications that are impractical now.

Using Jaskell

Most new computers now come with multiple processors. The laptop on which I'm writing this has a dual-core chip, which means, from a software development standpoint, it is a multiprocessor machine. Running applications efficiently on machines that have multiple processors means writing good thread-safe code. Writing good thread-safe code is extraordinarily difficult. Even those of us who thought we knew what we were doing were mortified to read Brian Goetz's *Java Concurrency in Practice* (Addison-Wesley). In his book, Brian effectively demonstrates that writing robust thread-safe code in Java (and, by extension, in any imperative language) is very difficult indeed.

About five years ago, our users were perfectly content with the ugly, graphical-version-of-a-terminal-window web applications we were cranking out. Then the annoying coders at Google released Google Maps and Gmail and showed our users that web applications didn't have to suck. We had to up our game and start building better web applications. The same will happen with concurrency. We developers can afford to be blissfully ignorant about serious threading concerns now, but someone will come along and show that it's possible to utilize the capabilities of new machinery in innovative ways, and we'll all have to follow along. A collision is approaching, between the kinds of machines we will target with our applications and our ability to write the kinds of code required to run effectively on them. Why not take advantage of polyglot programming to simplify our task?

Functional languages don't suffer from many of the shortcomings of imperative languages. Functional languages adhere to mathematical principles more rigorously. For example, a function in a functional language works just like a function in mathematics: the output is entirely dependent on the input. In other words, functions can't modify external *state* as they do their work. Pure functional languages have no concept of a variable or statefulness. Of course, that isn't practical. However, there are some very good hybrid functional languages that have many of the desirable characteristics without serious usability constraints. Examples of functional languages include Haskell, OCaml, erlang, SML, and others.

In particular, functional languages handle multithreaded support much better than imperative languages because they discourage statefulness. The upshot of this is that is it easier to write robust thread-safe code in a functional language than in an imperative one.

Enter Jaskell, a version of the Haskell language that runs on the Java platform. In other words, it is a way to write Haskell code that produces Java byte code.[*]

Here is an example from the Jaskell site. Let's say you wanted to implement a class in Java that allowed safely accessing an element of an array. You could write a class that resembles the following:

```
class SafeArray{
    private final Object[] _arr;
    private final int _begin;
    private final int _len;

    public SafeArray(Object[] arr, int len){
        _arr = arr;
        _begin = begin;
        _len = len;
    }

    public Object at(int i){
        if(i < 0 || i >= _len){
            throw new ArrayIndexOutOfBoundsException(i);
        }
        return _arr[_begin + i];
    }

    public int getLength(){
        return _len;
    }
}
```

The same functionality may be written in Jaskell as a *tuple*, which is essentially an associative array:

---

[*] Download at *http://jaskell.codehaus.org/*.

```
newSafeArray arr begin len = {
  length = len;
  at i = if i < begin || i >= len then
            throw $ ArrayIndexOutOfBoundsException.new[i]
         else
            arr[begin + i];
}
```

Because tuples work as associative arrays, calling `newSafeArray.at(3)` calls the at portion of the tuple, which evaluates the code defined by that part of the tuple. Even though Jaskell isn't object-oriented, both inheritance and polymorphism may be simulated using tuples in Jaskell. And, some desirable behavior like the use of *mixins* is possible with tuples in Jaskell but not with the core Java language. Mixins offer an alternative to the combination of interfaces and inheritance, where you can inject code into a class, not just a signature, without using inheritance. This is possible today with Aspects and AspectJ (yet another language in our current polyglot mix).

Haskell (and therefore Jaskell) features lazy evaluation of functions, meaning that eventualities are never executed until needed. For example, this code is perfectly legal in Haskell but would never work in Java:

```
makeList = 1 : makeList
```

The code reads "Make a list with a single element. If more elements are needed, evaluate them as needed." This function essentially creates a never-ending list of 1's.

Of course, to take advantage of Haskell syntax (via Jaskell), someone on your development team must understand how Haskell works. Increasingly, just as we now have database administrators on projects, we'll have other specialists to write code that exhibits special characteristics. Perhaps you have a complex scheduling algorithm that would be 1,000 lines of Java code but only 50 of Haskell. Why not take advantage of the Java *platform* and write it in a language more suitable to the task?

This style of development introduces its own set of headaches that offset its benefits. Debugging multilingual applications is more difficult than debugging applications written in a single language: ask any developer who's had to debug the interaction between JavaScript and Java. The easiest solution to that problem in the future will be the same as it is now: rigorous unit testing, which eliminates time spent in the debugger.

Ola's Pyramid

The polyglot style of development will continue to lead us in the direction of domain-specific languages (DSLs) as well. In the near future, our language landscape will look very different: specialized languages will be used as the building blocks to create very specific DSLs that are in turn very close to the problem domains we are trying to solve. The era of single-use general-purpose languages is drawing to a close; we're entering a new realm of specialization. Maybe it's time to dust off that college Haskell textbook!

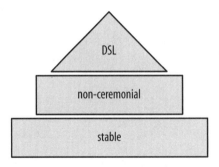

FIGURE 14-2. Ola's Pyramid

My colleague, Ola Bini, has added some nuance to this idea of polyglot programming, defining the new application stack. His view of the modern development world looks like Figure 14-2. This diagram suggests that we'll use a language (perhaps a statically typed language) for the *stability* layer, a more productive language (probably dynamic in nature, like JRuby, Groovy, or Jython) for day-to-day coding, and domain-specific languages (as discussed in "Fluent Interfaces" in Chapter 11) to align our code more closely to the needs of business analysts and end users. I think Ola has nailed the way that the disparate ideas of polyglot programming, domain-specific languages, and dynamic languages all fit together.

All doctors at one time were general practitioners, but as their field advanced, specialization became inevitable. Software complexity is quickly driving us toward specialization, both because of the types of applications we must write and the underlying platforms. To address this brave new world, we should embrace polyglot programming to provide more specialized tools for the platforms, and domain-specific languages to address increasingly difficult problem domains. Software development in the next five years will look very different than it does today!

CHAPTER FIFTEEN

Find the Perfect Tools

THROUGHOUT THE BOOK THUS FAR, I'VE SHOWN YOU HOW TO SOLVE VARIOUS PROBLEMS using a slew of different tools: batch files, bash scripts (both one-liners and full-blown scripts), Windows PowerShell, Ruby, Groovy, sed, awk, and a whole menagerie of big-eyed O'Reilly animals. Now the critical time has come. You've identified a problem that is causing grief and you want to automate it away: which tool do you use? The first tool you'll probably use is a lowly text editor. So, I'll start by talking about this perhaps most important tool in your arsenal.

The Quest for the Perfect Editor

Developers still spend a lot of time with plain text. No matter how many wizards and other sorcerers we develop, most coding is still in plain text. Most of the information you keep should also reside in plain text because you never know if the tool you are using will be around in five years. It's a good bet that you'll be able to read plain ASCII (and probably Unicode) for the next century or so. (As *The Pragmatic Programmer* [Addison-Wesley] admonishes: "Keep knowledge in plain text.")

Because so much of what we do revolves around text, it makes sense to find your perfect text editor. This isn't about IDEs; company policy and the language you use generally dictate that. IDEs are great at producing source code. But they are lacking in some of the best tools for plain old text.

I'll admit that I once had an editor fetish. I had a half dozen editors installed on my machine because I liked different features of each one. One day, I decided to create a list of all the things I thought a perfect editor should have, learn every nuance, and get out of the editor-of-the-day business forever.

> **NOTE**
> Find your perfect editor and learn it inside and out.

Here is my list. These are the things I think the perfect editor should have, along with the editors I've found that embody this ideal. Your list will probably differ.

Neal's List of What Makes a Perfect Editor

A macro recorder

Back in the olden days (a couple of decades ago), macros were one of the most important parts of a developer's arsenal. I still never go a full week without recording at least one. The advent of live templates in IDEs replaced a lot of the bread-and-butter tasks of macros. In fact, the most popular development environment for Java (the open source Eclipse) still doesn't have a macro recorder. If you had told a 1980s-era Unix programmer that a development tool existed that wouldn't let you record macros, he would have been horrified. (To be fair, the next version of Eclipse is supposed to grow this support.)

Record macros for all symmetrical text manipulation.

Macros are still a powerful tool, but you have to think about problems in certain ways. When you need to de-cruft some HTML you've harvested from source, or cruft up some code with HTML tags, you can record the operation on a single line and make sure you end up in the same place on the next line. That allows you to play back the macros on all subsequent lines.

The perfect editor should have readable macro syntax, so you can save common macros and reuse them. For example, the open source JEdit editor is written using BeanShell, a Java-like scripting language. Every time you record a macro in JEdit, it presents it in an open buffer for you to save it. Here is a macro recorded in JEdit that takes an HTML list of terms that is crammed onto a single line (because of display spacing issues) and expands it to one entry per line:

```
SearchAndReplace.setSearchString("<li>");
SearchAndReplace.setAutoWrapAround(false);
SearchAndReplace.setReverseSearch(false);
SearchAndReplace.setIgnoreCase(true);
SearchAndReplace.setRegexp(true);
SearchAndReplace.setSearchFileSet(new CurrentBufferSet());
SearchAndReplace.find(view);
textArea.goToPrevCharacter(false);
textArea.goToNextWord(false,false);
textArea.goToNextWord(false,false);
textArea.goToNextWord(false,false);
```

As you can see, BeanShell is quite readable, which encourages you to save useful recorded macros for future use.

Launchable from the command line

You should be able to launch the editor from the command line, passing single or multiple files. TextMate, one of the editors that made my list, goes one better. When launched in a directory, it automatically treats the directory as a project, showing all the files in the directory and its subdirectories in its project drawer.

Regular expression search and replace

Your editor should have robust regular expression support for both single and cross-file search and replace. Because we spend so much time with text, learning regular expression syntax is absolutely invaluable.

It can sometimes save literally days of work. There was once an event that convinced me of the power of regular expressions. I was working on a project that had over 1,000 Enterprise JavaBeans (EJB), and it was decided that all of the non-EJB methods (that is, all the methods except the EJB mandated callback methods) needed an extra parameter. It was estimated that it would take six days for someone to do this by hand (and the jockeying had already begun to *not* be the person to do it). One of the developers on the team knew regular expressions really well. He sat down with his trusty text editor (Emacs) and, two hours later, had done all the replacements. That was the day that I decided that I, too, needed to know regular expression syntax really well.

This is an example of the Expert Plumber phenomenon. Let's say you've hired a plumber to fix a problem in a large building. The expert plumber walks around with his hands in his pockets for several days, looking at all the plumbing fixtures in the building. At the end of the third day, he crawls under something and turns one valve. "That'll be $2,000, please." You stare dumbfounded: "$2,000? But you only turned one valve!" "Yep," he says. "$1 to turn the valve, $1,999 for knowing which valve to turn."

Good knowledge of regular expressions turns you into the developer equivalent of the expert plumber. In the situation I just cited, the developer took an hour and 58 minutes getting the syntax just right, then less than two minutes to actually run it. To the untrained eye, he spent most of that time not being very productive (that is, fighting with regular expression syntax), but in the end, he saved days' worth of work.

> **NOTE**
> Good knowledge of regular expressions can save orders of magnitude of effort.

Additive cut and copy commands

Inexplicably, most modern IDEs have only a single clipboard with a single entry. Really good editors give you not only *cut* and *copy* but also *copy append* and *cut append* commands, which append the text to the existing text on the clipboard. This allows you to build up contents on the clipboard instead of making round trips from source to destination (all too often, I see developers *copy*, switch, *paste*, switch, *copy*, switch, *paste*, etc.). It is much more efficient to do all your copying in the source file, then switch to the destination to paste the completed text.

> **NOTE**
> Don't make round trips when you can batch.

Multiple registers

Editors that have additive *cut* and *copy* commands usually have multiple registers as well. This is really just the old-school name for multiple clipboards. In perfect editors, you get as many clipboards as keys on the keyboard. You can create multiple clipboards at the operating system–level (see "Clipboard(s)" in Chapter 2), but it's nice to have support right in your text editor as well.

Cross-platform

Having a cross-platform editor doesn't affect all developers, but anyone who must span more than one operating system (sometimes multiple times a day) should have a cross-platform Swiss army knife that can show up anywhere.

The Candidates

Here are some of the editors that meet most of the criteria I laid out earlier. This isn't meant to be an exhaustive list, but it's a good place to start.

VI

> Of course, this one had to make the list. Many of the advanced features mentioned above started with this editor and the ones it was based upon. VI is still around and going strong. The most popular cross-platform version is called VIM (for "VI Improved") and exists for all platforms. The only place where it falls a bit short is the readable macro syntax requirement. VI is incredibly hard to learn; it has a virtual cliff-face learning curve. But, once you've mastered it, you are the most effective manipulator of text possible. Watching experienced VI editors, people say that the cursor just follows their eyes. Of course, there is low-level warfare between the VI and Emacs crowds, but they are really different things: VI strives to be the ultimate text manipulation tool, and Emacs strives to be an IDE for whatever language you type in. VI wags say that "Emacs is a great operating system with rudimentary text editing support."

Emacs

> This is the other old-school editor that has a devoted (no, fanatical) following. It supports all the features listed above (if you count elisp, Emacs' macro language, as "readable"). It exists as Emacs, XEmacs (a graphical skin on Emacs for operating systems like Windows), and AquaEmacs (specifically for Mac OS X, it uses the native Mac OS X commands in addition to the traditional Emacs commands). Emacs is sometimes finger-twisting to get stuff done (some wags say that Emacs stands for "Escape Meta Alt Control Shift") but it packs a huge amount of power. It has "modes" for different languages, allowing sophisticated syntax highlighting, special-purpose tools, and a host of other behaviors. Emacs is in fact the prototype for modern IDEs.

JEdit

> I must admit that this one surprised even me. I had used JEdit for several years, then kind of wandered away. But, as I was putting my list together, I reevaluated JEdit and it meets every criteria on the list. It has become a very capable editor, with a host of plug-ins that allow it to utilize lots of third-party tools (like Ant) and support lots of languages. It is built on top of BeanShell, meaning that it is easy to customize and modify, especially for Java developers.

TextMate (and eEditor)

> TextMate is an editor for Mac OS X that has won lots of hearts and minds (including stealing some of the famously Emacs-centric users). It is very powerful in unobtrusive ways, supports most of the items on the list above, and plays very nicely with Mac OS X. While it initially failed the cross-platform requirement, it has become so popular on Mac OS X that another company is porting it to Windows (calling it eEditor).

Choosing the Right Tool for the Job

In his book *The Paradox of Choice* (Harper Perennial), Barry Schwartz cites a study showing that users are paralyzed by too many choices. Rather than being happy that they have lots of choices, too many choices make them uncomfortable. For example, there was a store that sold jam, and to allow customers to sample their wares, they put out a table with three jars of jam. Sales of jam skyrocketed because customers liked being able to taste the jam before they bought it. Using logic, the proprietors decided to put out 20 jars of jam for tasting. And the sales of jam plummeted. Having three jars was good because people liked to be able to sample. But having 20 jars became overwhelming. People still sampled jam, but there were so many choices, it paralyzed their decision-making process, leading to fewer jam sales.

We software developers have the same issue when it comes time to solve a problem: there are so many ways to attack it, we are sometimes prevented from even starting. For example, in the SqlSplitter example created to bust SQL files into smaller chunks cited in "Build a SQL Splitter in Ruby" (Chapter 4), the developer with whom I was pair-programming initially thought about using *sed, awk*, C#, and even Perl to try to solve the problem, but quickly realized that it would take too long. Given the number of choices we have, how do you pick?

Increasingly, I've been leaning on what I call "real" scripting languages for more and more of my automation chores. By that, I mean a general-purpose language that supports scripting but has the kind of heavy-duty support of a general-purpose language. You can never tell when a little "jig" or "shim" will grow up to be a real part of your project. Useful little utilities that you create one day to handle some little chore have a way of sticking around, gradually growing new functionality as you need to do more stuff. At some point, it graduates into a real part of your project, and you'll want to start applying the same kinds of rigor to it as your "real" code (like version control, unit testing, refactoring, etc.). Examples of "real" scripting languages include Ruby, Python, Groovy, Perl, etc.

> NOTE
> Use a "real" scripting language for automation chores.

Refactoring SqlSplitter for Testablility

Back in "Build a SQL Splitter in Ruby" in Chapter 4, I described an automation solution for breaking a large SQL file into smaller chunks, called SqlSplitter. We thought we would need to perform this trick only one time, but it "accidentally" became an important part of our project. Because we wrote it in Ruby, it was easy for it to transition from "shim" to actual asset, including the code hygiene usually reserved for real pieces of projects (like unit testing). For the SqlSplitter class, it is easy to refactor it a bit so that you can write unit tests for it. Here is the updated version:

```
class SqlSplitter
  attr_writer :sql_lines❶
```

```
def initialize(output_path, input_file)
  @output_path, @input_file = output_path, input_file
end

def make_a_place_for_output_files
  Dir.mkdir(@output_path) unless @output_path.nil? or File.exists? @output_path
end

def lines_o_sql❷
  @sql_lines.nil? ? IO.readlines(@input_file) : @sql_lines
end

def create_output_file_from_number(file_number)
  file = File.new(@output_path + "chunk " + file_number.to_s + ".sql",
      File::CREAT|File::TRUNC|File::RDWR, 0644)
end

def generate_sql_chunks
  make_a_place_for_output_files
  line_num = 1
  file_num = 0
  file = create_output_file_from_number(1)
  found_ending_marker, seen_1k_lines = false
  lines_o_sql.each do |line|❸
    file.puts(line)
    seen_1k_lines = (line_num % 1000 == 0) unless seen_1k_lines
    line_num += 1
    found_ending_marker = (line.downcase =~ /^\W*go\W*$/ or
        line.downcase =~ /^\W*end\W*$/) != nil
    if seen_1k_lines and found_ending_marker
      file.close
      file_num += 1
      file = create_output_file_from_number(file_num)
      found_ending_marker, seen_1k_lines = false
    end
  end
  file.close
end
end
```

❶ Add an attr_writer for the sql_lines member variable. This allows you to inject a test value into the class after construction but before you call any of the methods.

❷ The lines_o_sql method abstracts the internal representation of the member variable, making sure that it has a value whenever it is called. None of the other methods needs to know anything about the internal workings of how the sql_lines member variable is populated.

❸ Using the method to iterate over the collection of source lines allows you to inject your own array of lines for testing rather than always relying on an input file.

Once the code is restructured, it is easy to write unit tests for it, as shown here:

```
require "test/unit"
require 'sql_splitter'
require 'rubygems'
require 'mocha'

class TestSqlSplitter < Test::Unit::TestCase
  OUTPUT_PATH = "./output4tests/"
```

```
private
def lots_o_fake_data❶
  fake_data = Array.new
  num_of_lines_of_fake_data = rand(250) + 1
  1.upto 250  do
    1.upto num_of_lines_of_fake_data do
      fake_data << "Lorem ipsum dolor sit amet."
    end
    fake_data << (num_of_lines_of_fake_data % 2 == 0 ? "END" : "GO")
    num_of_lines_of_fake_data = rand(250) + 1
  end
  fake_data
end

public
def test_mocked_out_dir
  ss = SqlSplitter.new("dummy_path", "dummy_file")
  Dir.expects(:mkdir).with("dummy_path")❷
  ss.make_a_place_for_output_files_in(dir)
end

def test_that_output_directory_is_created_correctly❸
  ss = SqlSplitter.new(OUTPUT_PATH, nil)
  ss.make_a_place_for_output_files
  assert File.exists? OUTPUT_PATH
end

def test_that_lines_o_sql_has_lines_o_sql❹
  lines = %w{Lorem ipsum dolor sit amet consectetur}
  ss = SqlSplitter.new(nil, nil)
  ss.sql_lines = lines
  assert ss.lines_o_sql.size > 0
  assert_same ss.lines_o_sql, lines
end

def test_generate_sql_chunks❺
  ss = SqlSplitter.new(OUTPUT_PATH, nil)
  ss.sql_lines = lots_o_fake_data
  ss.generate_sql_chunks
  assert File.exists? OUTPUT_PATH
  assert Dir.entries(OUTPUT_PATH).size > 0
  Dir.entries(OUTPUT_PATH).each do |f|
    assert f.size > 0
  end
end

def teardown
  `rm -fr #{OUTPUT_PATH}` if File.exists? OUTPUT_PATH
end
end
```

❶ This generates an array of data that looks kind of like SQL but has the markers that you need (that is, "GO" and "END").

❷ This uses Mocha, the Ruby mocking library, to mock out the directory creation for testing purposes.

❸ This tests that the output directory is created correctly.

❹ This tests that the `lines_o_sql` method does return an array consisting of the strings passed into the `sql_lines` mutator.

❺ This is the primary test. It tests that the `SqlSplitter` class generates output files based on parsing the input (or something that looks like the input).

This version tests all aspects of the `SqlSplitter`, including mocking out the filesystem so that you can test that it interacts with the underlying operating system correctly. Because this is Ruby code, I was able to run rcov, the code coverage tool, to verify that I have 100 percent test coverage (see Figure 15-1). This is important for scripts, especially for edge cases that come up only occasionally.

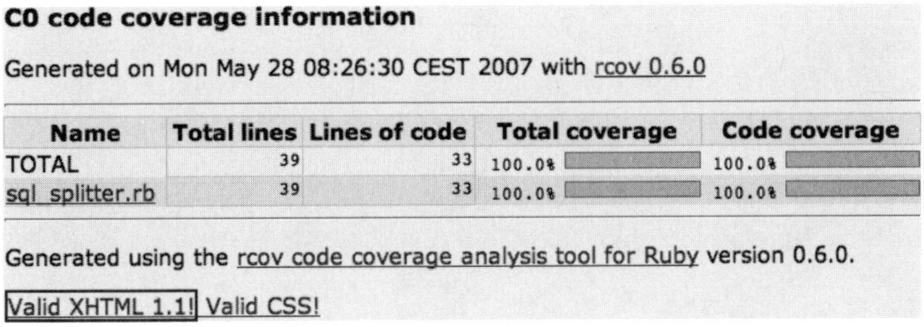

C0 code coverage information

Generated on Mon May 28 08:26:30 CEST 2007 with rcov 0.6.0

Name	Total lines	Lines of code	Total coverage	Code coverage
TOTAL	39	33	100.0%	100.0%
sql_splitter.rb	39	33	100.0%	100.0%

Generated using the rcov code coverage analysis tool for Ruby version 0.6.0.

Valid XHTML 1.1! Valid CSS!

FIGURE 15-1. Code coverage for SqlSplitter

This code did not originally have tests, but it was deemed important enough later to start treating this little utility as real code. One of the serious disadvantages of command-line tools like *bash, sed, awk,* and others is the lack of testability. Of course, you generally don't need to test these types of utilities...until you really, really need to test them. One of the main disadvantages of Ant is the lack of testability as Ant files grow to thousands of lines of "code" (sorry, I still can't bring myself to call XML *code*). Because Ant is XML, you can't easily *diff* it or refactor it (although some IDEs support limited refactoring), or perform any of the other code hygiene natural to "real" languages.

Nothing prevents someone from writing a unit test for a bash script, but it would be difficult at best. No one ever thinks about testing command-line tools because they don't think the tools are sophisticated enough to warrant it. They almost always start out too simple to test, but grow into hard-to-debug-yet-critical-to-the-project behemoths.

Keeping Behavior in Code

A ubiquitous part of most "enterprise" development is XML. In fact, some projects have as much XML as they do "real" code. XML started its intrusion into the development world for two reasons. First, it is easy to parse, with lots of standard libraries around that make it easy to produce and consume. This is the main reason that it took over the usage of Unix-style "little languages" (the configuration files that configure the various parts of Unix). The second reason is the realization that one of the best ways to leverage reusable code is via frameworks. And frameworks have two fundamental parts: the framework code itself and the configuration that allows you to drive the framework. It is frequently handy for the configuration part to have *late binding*: the ability to change the code without having to recompile the application. That was a huge selling point of the early versions of EJB, the ability for specialized deployment experts to tweak the transaction characteristics of your EJB. That sounds a bit ludicrous now, but it sounded cool back then. But the efficacy of configuration kept in a late-bound configuration is still a useful idea.

The problem with XML? It's not real code, but it pretends to be. XML has limited refactoring, it's hard to write, it's hideous to try to *diff* two XML files, and it has weak support for things that we take for granted in a computer language (like variables).

Fortunately, we can solve problems with XML by generating it rather than writing it by hand. The modern dynamic languages all have markup builders, with specific ones to build XML. Here's an example. The *struts-config.xml* file exists in every Struts project (if you aren't familiar with Struts, it's a popular web application framework for Java). The configuration file allows you to configure, among other things, database connection pools. That snippet of the *struts-config* file looks like this:

```
<data-sources>
    <data-source
            type="com.mysql.jdbc.jdbc2.optional.MysqlDataSource">
        <set-property property="url"
            value="jdbc:mysql://localhost/schedule" />
        <set-property property="user" value="root" />
        <set-property property="maxCount" value="5" />
        <set-property property="driverClass"
            value="com.mysql.jdbc.Driver" />
        <set-property value="1" property="minCount" />
    </data-source>
</data-sources>
```

What if we want the minimum number of connections to always be 5 less than the maximum number of connections? Because this is XML, we don't have a good variable mechanism, so we have to manage this by hand, which is, of course, prone to errors. Consider this version of the same snippet of XML, but kept in a Groovy markup builder instead:

```
def writer = new StringWriter()
def xml = new MarkupBuilder(writer)
def maxCount = 10
def countDiff = 4

xml.'struts-config'() {
  'data-sources'() {
    'data-source'(type:'com.mysql.jdbc.jdbc2.optional.MysqlDataSource') {
      'set-property'(property:'url', value:'jdbc:mysql://localhost/schedule')
      'set-property'(property:'user', value:'root')
      'set-property'(property:'maxCount', value:"${maxCount}")
      'set-property'(property:'driverClass', value:'com.mysql.jdbc.Driver')
      'set-property'(property:'minCount', value:"${maxCount - countDiff}")
    }
```

```
    }
    // . . .
```

Markup builders allow you to write structured code that has the same hierarchical structure as the XML it generates, using parameters and name/value pairs to generate XML attributes and child elements. This is easier to read because it has much less XML-based noise in it, like curly braces. But the real benefit to having this structure in code is the ease with which you can create derived values with variables. In this example, minCount is based on maxCount, meaning you never have to synchronize the values by hand. Using the Groovy Ant task, you can include this builder file as part of your build process, autogenerating your XML configuration every time you perform a build.

OK, but what if you already have a *struts-config.xml* file and don't want to retype it to get it into a builder? Easy: unbuild it. Here is the Groovy code that takes an existing XML file and converts it to Groovy builder code:

```
import javax.xml.parsers.DocumentBuilderFactory
import org.codehaus.groovy.tools.xml.DomToGroovy

def builder     =
    DocumentBuilderFactory.newInstance().newDocumentBuilder()
def inputStream = new FileInputStream("../struts-config.xml")
def document    = builder.parse(inputStream)
def output      = new StringWriter()
def converter   = new DomToGroovy(new PrintWriter(output))

converter.print(document)
println output.toString()
```

Ruby has similar builders, with the same capabilities (in fact, the Ruby builders were inspired by the Groovy builders). Using builders to generate code allows you all the facilities to which developers have grown accustomed. Never write XML by hand; always generate it. Of course, it seems a little silly to generate and ungenerate XML. (Why not just remove the middleman XML, as Ruby has—most of the configuration in the Ruby world is done in Ruby code and YAML, which is really embedded Ruby code.) But you can't retrofit all the frameworks in languages like Java and C# overnight to use real code for configuration. At least you can write code that generates the XML, yielding the benefits of having behavior in code, and use the unbuilders to get it into code the first time.

> **NOTE**
> Keep behavior in (testable) code.

If you start all your automation projects out in a powerful scripting language, it allows you to make the call as to when it becomes invaluable to add the kind of infrastructure of real code. It also means that you don't have to learn an entire zoo of special-purpose tools. Scripting languages today give you virtually all the affordances of command-line tools.

Useful things tend to never go away. They keep growing and growing until they become an important part of your process. All little utilities reach a critical mass where they become important and thus deserving of real attention. If you build them right in the beginning, you won't have to rewrite them when that day comes. Try as much as you can to keep behavior in code (not in tools or markup languages like XML). We know all sorts of ways to deal with code: *diff* to compare versions, refactoring, robust testing libraries. Why would we give all the accumulated knowledge of what we know about code just for the siren song of some elaborate tool?

NOTE
Pay attention to the evolution of your tools.

Un-Choosing the Wrong Tools

As important (or perhaps even more so) than choosing the right tools is rejecting bad tools. In fact, an anti-pattern exists that describes this: *boat anchor*. A boat anchor is a tool that you are forced to use even though it is ridiculously ill-suited for the job at hand. Frequently, this boat anchor costs a vast amount of money, increasing the political pressure to use it for every situation. For a tortured but depressingly accurate metaphor, imagine that a carpenter was forced to use a sledge hammer (undoubtably powerful) for driving nails. The unsuitability in this case is obvious, but we make similar and even worse decisions in software.

I was recently involved in the inception of a project at a large enterprise. We were introducing many Agile tenets to the developers, who viewed them as fresh air. One of the decisions involved version control. The Infrastructure Control representative came to talk to us and provided two choices: Rational ClearCase or Serena Version Manager. In case you aren't familiar with these two version control packages, both are quite expensive and have vast functionality (with a corresponding footprint). Our choice? None of the above. We suggested Subversion, the lightweight open source version control package. We described it to the Infrastructure Control people, and they agreed that it sounded perfect for their needs. Then the big question "How much is the licensing fee per user?" They were stunned when we told them that it was free. Then, reflectively, they said, "You know, we installed ClearCase for another group of developers about six months ago, and they don't seem to like it very much."

Large companies get into an acquisition mode where they try to find one-size-fits-all tools for development. It makes sense for a large company to standardize on infrastructure. But at some point, the standard infrastructure becomes more of an impediment than a benefit. This is especially true for overly complex tools. In fact, I've coined a term for it: *complexitax*. Complexitax is the extra cost that you pay for accidental complexity introduced by a tool that does more than you need. Lots of projects drown in complexity imposed by the tools that developers buy, ironically almost always to improve productivity.

NOTE
Pay as little complexitax as you can.

How do you successfully fight boat anchors and boat anchor policies? Here are some strategies for attacking needless complexity. Waging effective campaigns against the governors on development makes the topics covered in Chapter 9 work.

Demonstrate simpler solutions

The corporate CIO's rationale makes sense to him: if we can standardize on a small set of tools, we don't have to do as much training, we can have people cross projects more easily, etc. Unfortunately, software vendors attack him with golf outings (one of my colleagues, any time he sees an unused boat anchor sitting in a corner, always says, "I hope that was a good golf outing"), relentless sales campaigns, and whatever else it takes to get him to buy their product. You can successfully battle the standard boat anchor by demonstrating that a much simpler thing fits this particular project much better. Start a little skunk works project on the side that shows that, for this simple web application, Tomcat actually works better than Websphere because we want to be able to script the deployment, which is easier on Tomcat.

Sometimes it is difficult to even get to the point where you can demonstrate one thing is better, especially if it takes a while to get it in place. Don't be ashamed to resort to begging; getting your way can save you massive amounts of time on an ongoing basis.

It's better to ask forgiveness than permission

One of my friends, Jared Richardson, had the difficult job of making one of the world's largest software companies more agile. He looked around and noticed that broken nightly builds were one of its biggest problems. Instead of escalating a request up the corporate hierarchy to get permission to set up CruiseControl on some of the projects, he just found an old desktop machine that no one was using and installed CruiseControl on it. He set it up to run continuous builds on several of the most troublesome projects. And he set it up to notify the developers via email any time they checked in code that broke the build. For the next few days, the developers all started asking him how to turn off the email notifications of broken builds. "Simple," he said, "Don't break the build." Eventually, they realized that was the only way to stop the pestering, so they cleaned up their code.

The company went from only three successful nightly builds a month to only three broken nightly builds a month. Some savvy manager looked around and said, "OK, something caused this—what was it?" That company now has the largest install base of CruiseControl in the world.

Use the Judo approach

Judo is a martial art that encourages practitioners to use their opponents' weight against them. We were on a project for a large company that had standardized on a particularly toxic version control package, and it was company-wide policy to use it. We tried it, but it was antithetical to the style of development we were doing. We needed to be able to check in very early and very often, without locking files (which makes it hard to refactor aggressively). The version control just couldn't handle it, so we used that fact against it. It harmed our workflow and therefore made us measurably less productive.

We reached a compromise. They allowed us to use Subversion, which was ideally suited to our job. To adhere to the company policy, we created a scheduled task that ran every night at 2 A.M. that did a checkout from our Subversion repository and checked that snapshot into the corporate version control. They got their code in the standard place, and we got to use the tool best suited for our work.

Fight internal feature creep and boat anchors

While vendors are the pushers of accidental complexity, it grows within organizations as well. Boat anchors don't have to be external tools; they are often existing, homegrown headaches. Lots of projects are saddled with inappropriate internal frameworks and tools (victims of the Standing on the Shoulders of Midgets anti-pattern). Business users request "nice to have" functionality without understanding the orders of magnitude of difficulty involved. Developers, architects, and tech leads must make users and management understand the cost of complexity incurred by using inappropriate tools, libraries, and frameworks.

Being saddled with an inappropriate tool may seem like a minor thing (especially to nondevelopers), but it can have a huge impact on the overall productivity of developers. A cut on the roof of your mouth isn't fatal, but the constant low-grade irritation keeps you from concentrating on important things. Inappropriate tools do the same thing. And overly complex inappropriate tools make it worse because you spend so much time dealing with the irrelevancies of the tool, you can't get real work done.

CHAPTER SIXTEEN

Conclusion: Carrying on the Conversation

PROGRAMMING IS A UNIQUE BEHAVIOR, NO MATTER HOW MUCH WE TORTURE METAPHORS TO compare it to other activities and professions. It combines engineering and craft in highly coupled ways, requiring good developers to exhibit a wide variety of skills: analytical thinking; extreme attention to detail on multiple levels and aesthetics; an awareness of macro and micro level concerns simultaneously; and a keen, fine-grained understanding of the subject matter we're writing software to assist. Ironically, developers have to understand business processes at a much lower level than the actual practitioners of the business. Business people can use their experience to make on-the-fly decisions when novel situations pop up; we must encode everything in algorithms and explicit behavior.

The original vision for *The Productive Programmer* was to provide a long list of recipes for productivity. It morphed into a two-part book, where the first part deals with the mechanics of productivity and the second concentrates on the practices of productivity as a developer. In its final form, this book still contains a fair number of recipes. But following recipes leaves you with tasty dishes, but no capability to create your own recipes. Identifying the mechanical productivity principles (acceleration, focus, automation, and canonicality) provided a nomenclature for recognizing new techniques that I never thought about. In essence, I wanted to create a cookbook that also shows you how to create your own recipes.

Part II, Practice, was designed to make you think about building software in ways that perhaps you hadn't before. Developers sometimes fall into ruts, necessitating a third party to come along and point out new ways of thinking. Hopefully, Part II did that.

In effect, the meta-goal of this book is to create a *dialogue*, not a monologue, about productivity at both the mechanics level and the practices level. I want to raise the awareness of how we as developers can become more productive. At the same time, I want other, much smarter people to carry on this conversation. Collectively, we can come up with a lot of amazingly cool stuff.

This means there can never be a comprehensive book about either aspect of productivity: it's a constantly changing landscape. To spur dialogue based on the monologue I've just created, I host a public wiki at *http://productiveprogrammer.com*. Every time you find something that makes you more productive, tell everyone else. When you discover a pattern (or anti-pattern) for productivity, publish it. The only way to continuously improve our productivity as a group is to collaborate, share war stories, and discover new stuff.

Come on over and let's continue the conversation.

APPENDIX

Building Blocks

Command lines are wonderful things. If you know the magical commands, the command line is usually the quickest route from intention to execution. Once upon a time, developers had no choice—they had to learn all the incantations by heart, and computer magazines filled up with all the interesting nuances of how DOS worked (and frequently, didn't work). When Windows conquered the users' desktops, the developers followed, and only us "seasoned" developers knew how to use the real dark magic under the skin.

Even though IDEs make novice developers more productive, the most productive developers still rely, even thrive, on this command-line Judo. Automating tasks through scripting, linking the inputs and outputs of existing tools, and performing small tasks on local and remote files is still best done at the blinking cursor. But first, you have to make sure you have the *right* blinking cursor. If you are on Unix or Mac OS X, you can skip the next section. If you are on Windows, you desperately need to read it.

Cygwin

As a Windows user, have you ever gotten jealous of the sheer amount of *stuff* that comes with a Linux distribution? Compilers for a dozen languages, debuggers, text editors, drawing tools, web servers, databases, publishing tools…the list goes on and on. You can have all that on top of Windows,[*] too—thanks to Cygwin.

Cygwin is a combination of several things:

- A Linux API emulation layer, allowing you to compile and run all those cool Linux programs.
- A collection of all those really great Unix-like tools.
- An installer/program manager for keeping the whole thing up-to-date.

First, download the Cygwin installer from *http://www.cygwin.com*. This is more than just an installer: it is a complete *package management system*. Even after you install Cygwin, you should keep this around; you will need it to install, update, and remove packages in the future. The installer you download is very small (about 300k), but that is just the tip of the iceberg— it will download a lot of stuff, potentially hundreds of megabytes depending on what options you decide to install (you won't need to install that much to run the examples in the book). For the bandwidth-impaired, you can purchase install CDs for a minimal fee.

The Cygwin installer is a bit odd to most Windows users' eyes. The package selection screen shows you a bunch of stuff to install, and each one can be selected for installation, upgrade,

---

[*] Of course, Mac users have access to all this stuff too. If the Unix tool you are looking for isn't already included in OS X, Mac users have the same ability to download source and build or use a package manager such as Fink or MacPorts to install tools.

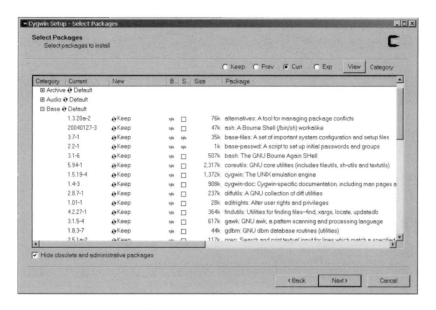

FIGURE A-1. The Cygwin installer is actually a package manager

or removal independently. At first, this is a little confusing; it helps if you keep in mind that this is a "package manager," not just an "installer."

Next, you have to make choices involving DOS versus Unix line endings. The short answer for the purpose of this book is to select Unix, but the reasons are more arcane. There are invisible characters at the end of every line, and the order of these invisible characters is different between DOS and Unix. Since you are installing Unix tools on your machine, you are now going to have DOS and Unix files on the same filesystem. By choosing Unix here, you might occasionally open a file and see '^M' at the end of every line. But if you choose DOS, you will run into potentially odder issues with all these tools that expect Unix line endings. From a practical standpoint, most applications today (except really terrible, old software like Windows Notepad) handle the distinction for you.

Finally, DOS and Unix have different path formats. On Windows, you might find a file at *c:\Documents and Settings\nford*, while on Unix, a path looks like */home/nford'*. Because Cygwin sits atop the Windows filesystem, in Cygwin you might know a file as */home/nford/ readme.txt*, but in Windows it is at *c:\cygwin\home\nford\readme.txt*. There are tools for converting one path type to another in Cygwin; occasionally a program will expect a certain format, and you'll have to know how to make them interchangeable.

When installing Cygwin, you will be presented with a list of all the stuff that is available. Browse through the categories and take a look at all the goodies. You will find text editors, databases, several shells, web servers, languages like Ruby and Python, and tons of other stuff. For the purposes of this book, start with the defaults (plus make sure that *wget* is also selected), and let it go. It will take a while to download and install everything.

Once it does, you should have a Cygwin shortcut, beckoning you to the Windows version of the bash shell.

The Command Line

Why is the command line so useful, especially in the Unix world? Why do all the Unix geeks get all misty eyed when they talk about it, and drool into their Birkenstocks? It goes back to the philosophy that the Unix creators built into the command line. They wanted a powerful set of tools that you could mix and match to form powerful composites. To that end, they built everything around a simple concept: streams of plain text. Virtually all the Unix command-line tools produce and consume plain text. Even text files can be converted into a stream of plain text (via the *cat* command) and put back into a file with the *redirection* command, the *>*.

For a simple example, you can take regular text with the *echo* command and pipe it through something that converts it from lowercase to uppercase (using the *tr*, or translate, command). This understands character classes (like *:lower:* and *:upper:*) like this (note that the $ isn't part of the command, the command-line prompt, left there so you can tell input from output):

```
$ echo "productively lazy" | tr "[:lower:]" "[:upper:]"
PRODUCTIVELY LAZY
```

The concept worth noticing here is the *pipe* command (the / character). It takes the output of the *echo* command and passes it into the *tr* command, which dutifully translates lowercase characters into uppercase ones. All Unix commands are wired this way, where the output of one becomes the input of the next. You can also create a file with that content by redirecting the output of this command into a file:

```
$ echo "productively lazy" | tr "[:lower:]" "[:upper:]" >pl.txt
$ cat pl.txt
PRODUCTIVELY LAZY
```

And, of course, you can take text from one file, do something to it, and put it into another file:

```
$ cat pl.txt | tr "[:upper:]" "[:lower:]" | tr "z" "Z" > plz.txt
productively laZy
```

Here is a more practical example. Suppose I have a large Java project with a bunch of classes that are "helpers" for other classes, and follow a naming convention of *Class* Helper, for the class it is helping. I want to find them all, even though they are scattered all over my project:

```
$ find . -name *Helper.java
```

And my army of trained minions dutifully responds:

```
./src/java/org/sample/domain/DomainHelper.java
./src/java/org/sample/gui/WindowHelper.java
./src/java/org/sample/logic/DocumentHelper.java
./src/java/org/sample/logic/GenericHelper.java
```

```
./src/java/org/sample/logic/LoginHelper.java
./src/java/org/sample/logic/PersistenceHelper.java
```

OK, fine, you can get the same result in the search dialog of an IDE. But the interesting thing about the command line is what you can do after you get these results. In an IDE, the results of that search are going to be in a window, and if you are lucky, you might be able to copy them out and paste them someplace. But from the command line, you can pipe that output into another tool. In this case, that tool is *wc. wc* is a tool that counts things; it can count words, characters, lines, and files:

```
$ find . -name *Helper.java | wc -l
6
```

The *wc -l* line simply counts the number of lines passed into it:

WHO NAMES THESE THINGS?

The Unix commands are very terse. After all, they were designed to work on teletype terminals and reward those who learn their way through their terseness. Once you learn them, it takes very little typing to get cool stuff to happen. But what about *grep*? Where did that come from?

Rumor has it that the *grep* command comes to us because of the search command in the *ex* editor. The *ex* editor was the line-based precursor to VI, the legendary Unix editor with the steepest imaginable learning curve. In *ex*, to perform a search, you entered command mode and typed *g* for global search, started a regular expression with the / character, typed your regular expression, terminated it with another /, and then told *ex* to print the result with a *p*. In other words, *g/re/p*. That was so common amongst Unix types that it became a verb. So, when it came time to write a search utility for the command line, they already had the perfect name: *grep*.

I know some of the helpers are actually subclasses of other helpers. I can already use *find* to find all of the helpers; now I want to look inside those files and find just those that happen to extend other helpers. For that, we use *grep*. We'll look at three differently nuanced versions of using the combination of *find* and *grep*. The first uses *find*'s extensive options:

```
$ find . -name *Helper.java -exec grep -l "extends .*Helper" {} \;
./src/java/org/sample/logic/DocumentHelper.java
./src/java/org/sample/logic/LoginHelper.java
```

What's going on in this incantation? See Table A-1 for a breakdown.

TABLE A-1. Decoding command-line magic

Character(s)	What it's doing
find	Execute the *find* command.
.	From the current directory.
-name	Matching name of "*Helper.java".

Character(s)	What it's doing
-exec	Execute the following command on each found file.
grep	*grep* command.
-l	Show the files with matching lines.
"extends .*Helper"	Match the regular expression for lines matching "extends" + a single space + zero or more characters + "Helper".
{}	The placeholder for the filename found by *find*.
\;	Terminate the command after -exec. Because this is a Unix command, you might want to pipe the results of this into another command, and the *find* command has to know when the "exec" is done.

Wow, that's a lot of bang for the buck in a compact syntax. Which is, of course, the point. Just to prove that many ways exist to do everything on a Unix command line, here is an alternative version that produces the same results, using the *xargs* command:

```
$ find . -name *Helper.java | xargs grep -l "extends .*Helper"
./src/java/org/sample/logic/DocumentHelper.java
./src/java/org/sample/logic/LoginHelper.java
```

Most of this one is the same, except that we're piping the output of the *find* command through *xargs*, which is a helper utility that will take the input from a pipe and place it at the end of its argument. Like the {} placeholder above, *xargs* will take the filenames produced by the *find* command and put them as the last parameter of the *grep* command. You can also use options for the *xargs* command to put the parameters that come through the pipe at different locations within the argument string. For example, the following command copies all the filenames that start with a capital letter to the *dest* directory:

```
$ ls -1d [A-Z]* | xargs -J % cp -rp % destdir
```

The *-J* flag tells *xargs* to use the % as the placeholder for the input coming through the pipe. This allows you to specify any replacement character you like, to ensure it doesn't conflict with some other character required by the target command.

Here's one last version of our *find* command:

```
$ grep -l "extends .*Helper" `find . -name *Helper.java`
./src/java/org/sample/logic/DocumentHelper.java
./src/java/org/sample/logic/LoginHelper.java
```

Notice those little backtick characters (`). We aren't using the pipe to send the output of one command to another—if we did that, *grep* would simply look through the list of filenames, not the content of the files themselves. Wrapping the find command in the backtick character (typically found at the upper left of U.S. keyboards) will make *find* execute first, and pass the output to *grep* as the *list of files* to search instead of the actual text to search.

Now, I glue together all of the stuff seen so far:

```
$ grep -l "extends .*Helper" `find . -name *Helper.java` | wc -l
2
```

While the individual commands were pretty trivial, with the *pipe* and the *backtick*, I can combine them in ways their original authors might not have anticipated (and that is a major philosophical point behind Unix). With the knowledge of a dozen commands or so, you too can look like a Unix power user. More importantly, you can slice and dice your projects in ways that just are not available from the menus inside of IDEs.

Getting Help When You Need It

In most cases, there is help available directly from the command line, but it can be a little cryptic and/or difficult to find at times. There are two basic ways to get help on any Unix-like system. The first is directly from the command itself. In most cases, you can simply type *--help* or *-h*, like this:

```
$ ls --help
```

The second way is the help system included in most Unix-like systems, the "Manual Pages (manpages)," which is accessed with the command *man <the thing you want help for>*, like this:

```
$ man wget
```

The third way is similar to the *man* command and available on most flavors of Linux, the *info* command. Like *man*, you can just type the name of the command you want help with, but unlike *man*, you can type *info* without a specific topic in mind to begin browsing.

Unfortunately, for most of the available built-in help, you have to at least know enough of what command you are seeking help for. Unix commands are often cryptic enough for this to be rare; for instance, you wouldn't think, "I need to know how to find out which files have references to my home directory in them. I know—I'll type *man grep*!" For this kind of help, nothing beats a good intro, cookbook, or shell reference manual.

INDEX

Symbols

80-10-10 Rule, 137

A

acceptance testing
    web applications, 58
accidental properties
    Aristotle on, 136
Alt-Tab viewer (Windows)
    history, 24
analysis (see byte code analysis; source analysis;
        static analysis)
Angry Monkey and Cargo Cults, 144
Ant
    non-build tasks, 56
anti-objects, 147
Aristotle
    on accidental and essential properties, 136
arrays (see zero-based arrays)
attributes, xiii
    (see also sticky attributes)
    searching by, 42
autocompletion
    Windows address bar, 20
automation, 52–68
    Ant, Nant and Rake, 56
    bash shell, 60
    batch files, 61
    caching locally, 53
    deleting downloads in Mac OS X, 62
    justifying, 65–67
    reinventing wheels, 53
    RSS feeds, 54
    Selenium with web pages, 58
    SqlSplitter, 64
    Subversion, 62
    web site interaction, 54
    yak shaving, 67
Automator (Mac OS X), 62

B

background
    problem solving, 147
balloon tips (Windows), 39
Bash Here context menu, 28
bash shell
    Cygwin, 28
    harvesting exception counts, 60
    retrieving files, 56
batch files
    Automator, 62
    retrieving files, 56
behavior
    generated code, 85
    testable code, 185
binaries
    version control, 71
Bini, Ola
    on polyglot programming, 173
blogs (see RSS feeds)

boat anchor
    antipattern, 186
build machines, 72
Buildix, 53
bundles
    TexMate, 78
byte code analysis, 110–112

C

caching
    locally, 53
Calendar (Java)
    citizenship, 126
calendars
    "meetings" for quiet time, 40
canonicality, 70–94
    build machines, 72
    defined, 70
    DRY documentation, 88–92
    DRY impedance mismatches, 80–88
    DRY version control, 70
    indirection, 73–80
    virtualization, 80
CheckStyle, 114
chere command, 28
citizenship, 120–127
    Calendar (Java), 126
    constructors, 121
    encapsulation, 120
    static methods, 121–126
class diagrams, 91
CLCL, 23
clipboard stack
    software, 23
clipboards
    accelerators, 21
    using batches, 22
code, xiii
    (see also examples; generated code; reusable code)
    Cyclomatic Complexity, 103
    keeping in sync with schemas, 86
    TDD- versus non-TDD code, 102
    XML, 183
code coverage
    SqlSplitter, 183
    TDD, 105
code snippets
    defined, 78

sharing, 79
Colibri application launcher, 11
colors
    built-in focus, 47
command line, xiii
    (see also shells)
    graphical, 15
    launching editors from, 177
    power of, 194–197
    setup for, 47
    Subversion, 62
Command Prompt Explorer Bar (Windows)
    using, 26
Command Prompt Here (Windows), 28
command prompts
    using, 25
commands, xiii
    (see also specific command)
    cut and copy in editors, 178
    typing, 34
comments
    refactoring to methods, 103
compiled languages
    code coverage, 105
complexitax principle, 186
composed method, xiii
    (see also refactoring)
    SLAP, 156–160
concentration
    maintaining, 38
configuration
    canonical, 79
constructors
    citizenship, 121
    default, 147
context switching
    time eater, 22
continuous integration
    defined, 72
copy command, 178
copying and pasting
    evils of, 78
creeping featurism, 132
cross-platform support
    editors, 178
cURL, 54
cut command, 178
Cyclomatic Complexity, 103
Cygwin, xiii, 192

(see also Unix)
bash shell, 28

D

data mapping
  impedance mismatches, 81–86
database schemas, 92
dbDeploy
  impedance mismatches, 87
debugging
  with Selenium, 60
defaults
  constructors, 121, 147
deleting
  downloads in Mac OS X, 62
Demeter, Law of, 140
dependent objects
  TDD, 98
desktops (see virtual desktops)
diagrams, xiii
  (see also class diagrams)
  creating, 91
Dietzler's Law, 137
distractions, 38–40
documentation, xiii
  (see also living documentation)
  DRY, 88–92
  up-to-date, 88
domain-specific languages
  polyglot style development, 173
Don't repeat yourself (see DRY)
downloads
  deleting in Mac OS X, 62
DRY (Don't repeat yourself)
  impedance mismatches, 80–88
  version control, 70
duplication (see canonicality)
dynamic languages
  code coverage, 105
  static analysis, 116

E

E Text Editor, 78
e-commerce
  JEE example, 160–164
Eclipse
  keyboard shortcuts, 29
  sharing code snippets, 79
Eclipse plug-ins

indirection, 73
editors, 176–179
eEditor, 179
80-10-10 Rule, 137
Emacs
  about, 179
  configuration information, 79
Emma, 114
encapsulation
  breaking, 120
Enso application launcher, 11
entropy
  defined, 130
essential properties
  Aristotle on, 136
examples
  byte code analysis, 111
  composed method, 156
  data mapping with Groovy, 81
  dbDeploy, 87
  Flog, 117
  fluent interfaces, 146, 152–154
  Groovy and XML, 185
  initialization in Java, 167
  Jaskell, 172
  Java versus Groovy, 170
  Java's reflection, 150
  JEE e-commerce site, 160–164
  launching presentations with Rake, 57
  living documentation wiki, 89
  logs with bash, 60
  opening spreadsheets with Ruby, 52
  Rails migration, 86
  refactoring SqlSplitter, 180
  retrieving files with Ant, 56
  singleton design pattern, 122
  SLAP, 160
  SqlSplitter in Ruby, 64
  Struts, 184
  TDDing unit tests, 99–105
  XML, 184
Excel
  opening spreadsheets with Ruby example,
    52
exception counts
  bash shell, 60
Explorer (see Windows)
expression builders, 147
expressions (see regular expressions)

eye candy
    value of, 10

F

factoring, xiii
    (see also refactoring)
    composed method, 156
file hierarchies
    versus search, 41
find command, 196
find utilities, 43
FindBugs, 110
Finder (Mac OS X)
    keyboard shortcuts, 20
    versus Spotlight, 17
Flog, 117
flow
    state of, 38
fluent interfaces
    example, 152–154
    using, 145–147
folders, xiii
    (see also virtual folders)
    launching pads, 12
foreground
    problem solving, 147
Frameworks
    speculative development, 130
Full Screen mode (Microsoft Office), 29
functional languages
    advantages of, 172

G

generated code
    adding behavior to, 85
global variables
    creating, 123
GNU/Linux (see Linux; Unix)
Google Desktop Search, 41
graphical command line, 15
graphical environments
    usefulness of, 52
grep command
    combined with find utilities, 43
    origin of, 195
Groovy
    analysis, 117
    GString class, 154
    reflection in Java, 152

    relationship to Java, 170
    testing Java, 151
Growl (Mac OS X)
    notifications, 39
GString class, 154

H

hard target searching, 42–44
hotkeys
    conflicts with, 15

I

IDE, xiii
    (see also Eclipse; Emacs; IntelliJ; Selenium)
IDE (Integrated Development Environment)
    keyboard shortcuts, 29
impedance mismatches, 80–88
    data mapping, 81–86
    migrations, 86
indirection, 73
    canonical configuration, 79
    canonicality, 77
    syncing JEdit macros, 75
    TextMate bundles, 78
IntelliJ
    keyboard shortcuts, 30
interfaces (see fluent interfaces)

J

Jaskell
    polyglot programming, 171
Java
    80-10-10 Rule, 138
    naming conventions, 144
    polyglot programming, 166–173
    primitives, 139
    reflection and meta-programming, 150
    search versus navigation, 32
    testing with Groovy, 151
JavaBeans
    object validity, 147
JavaScript
    polyglot programming, 170
JDepend, 114
JEdit editor
    about, 179
    macros, 75
JEE e-commerce example, 160–164

Junction
    links for Windows, 76

K
Key Promoter plug-in (IntelliJ), 30
keyboards
    using, 29
    versus mouse, 29

L
Larry's Any Text File Indexer, 41
launchers, 10–18
    about, 10
    Linux, 18
    Mac OS X, 15
    Windows, 12
launching
    editors from the command line, 177
Launchy application launcher, 11
Law of Demeter, 140
laws (see Dietzler's Law; Law of Demeter)
length
    versus usefulness, 10
libraries
    version control, 71
Linux, xiii
    (see also Unix)
    launchers, 18
live templates, xiii
    (see also code snippets)
    IDEs, 31
living documentation
    subversion, 88
logs
    automating with bash example, 60

M
Mac OS X, xiii
    (see also Finder; Spotlight; Unix)
    command prompts, 26
    deleting downloads, 62
    killing instances of applications while Apple-
        Tabbing, 24
    launches, 15
    rooted views, 45
    virtual desktops, 48
macrco recorders
    editors, 176

macros
    JEdit, 75
    using, 33
maps (see tree maps)
meetings
    for quiet time, 40
meta-programming, 150–154
    fluent interface example, 152–154
    Java and reflection, 150
    testing Java with Groovy, 151
methods
    naming conventions for, 144
    refactoring comments to, 103
metrics
    Cyclomatic Complexity, 103
    static analysis, 113
mice (see mouse)
Microsoft Office
    Full Screen mode, 29
Microsoft Windows (see Windows)
migrations
    impedance mismatches, 86
mirroring
    web sites, 53
Monad (see Windows Power Shell)
monitors
    multiple, 48
mouse
    versus keyboard, 29
    versus typing, 18
    using, 29
My Documents (Windows)
    moving folder, 13

N
naming conventions
    test names versus method names, 144
Nant
    non-build tasks, 56
navigation
    versus search, 32, 40–42
    versus typing, 14
.NET
    framework, 131
    search versus navigation, 33
    Windows Power Shell, 61
notifications
    turning off, 39

O

objects (see anti-objects; dependent objects)
Occam, Sir William of, 137–140
operating systems (see Linux; Mac OS X;
         Windows; Unix)
optimistic revisions, 70
OS X (see Finder; Mac OS X; Spotlight; Unix)

P

PacMan
    foreground and background problem solving,
         148
Panopticode
    static analysis, 113
pbcopy and pbpaste commands, 27
philosophers, 136–142
    Aristotle, 136
    Law of Demeter, 140
    Occam's razor, 137–140
pipe command, 194
Pipes (see Yahoo! Pipes)
plug-ins
    Eclipse, 73
PMD, 112
polyglot programming, 166–174
    current trends, 169–173
    Java origins of, 166–169
    Ola's pyramid, 173
popd command, 25
PowerToys (Windows), xiii
    (see also Virtual Desktop Manager)
    about, 28
    download location, 13
primitives
    Java, 139
programming (see meta-programming)
project management
    with rooted views, 45
    virtual folders, 47
projects
    shortcuts, 47
pushd command, 25

Q

Quicksilver, 15
quiet time
    instituting, 40

R

Rake
    common tasks, 57
    migrations, 86
    non-build tasks, 56
recorder
    macros, 33
refactoring, xiii
    (see also composed method)
    comments to methods, 103
    composed method, 156
    keyboard shortcuts, 31
    SqlSplitter, 180
    XML, 183
reflection
    Java and meta-programming, 150
registers
    editors, 178
registry (Windows)
    autocompletion tweak for Windows 2000,
         20
    folders, 13
regular expressions
    in search, 43
remember history shell feature, 23
repetition (see canonicality)
Resharper
    search versus navigation, 33
reusable code
    refactoring to composed method, 159
rooted views
    using, 44
RSS feeds
    automating interaction with, 54
Ruby, xiii
    (see also Rake)
    SqlSplitter, 64

S

schemas, xiii
    (see also database schemas)
    keeping in sync with code, 86
    repeatable snapshots of changes, 87
search
    editors, 177
    hard target searching, 42–44
    versus navigation, 32, 40–42
servers

continuous integration, 72
service-oriented architecture (SOA)
    accidental versus essential complexity, 136
shells, xiii
    (see also bash shell; Windows Power Shell)
    remember history feature, 23
shortcuts
    project-based, 47
Simian, 115
Single Level of Abstraction Principle (see SLAP)
singleton design pattern, 122
SLAP (Single Level of Abstraction Principle),
        156–164
    composed method, 156–160
    JEE e-commerce example, 160–164
SOA (service-oriented architecture)
    accidental versus essential complexity, 136
source analysis, 112–113
Spotlight (Mac OS X), 17, 42
SQL
    polyglot programming, 169
SqlSplitter
    file in Ruby, 64
    refactoring, 180
stacks (see clipboard stack)
static analysis, 110–117
    byte code, 110–112
    dynamic languages, 116
    metrics, 113
    source analysis, 112–113
static methods
    citizenship, 121–126
sticky attributes, 46–47
Subversion
    command line, 62
    living documentation, 88
    wiki example, 88
syncing
    JEedit macros, 75

T

TDD (Test-Driven Development), 98–107
    code coverage, 105
    composed method, 160
    example, 99–105
technical documents (see documentation; living
        documentation)
templates (see code snippets; live templates)
Test-Driven Development (see TDD)

testing, xiii
    (see also acceptance testing; verification)
    Java with Groovy, 151
    naming conventions for, 144
    refactoring SqlSplitter, 180
TextMate bundles, 78
TextMate editor, 179
timebox development, 67
tree maps
    using, 115
triggers
    Quicksilver, 16
Tweak UI utility, 13
typing
    commands, 34
    versus mousing, 18
    versus navigation, 14

U

unit tests
    TDD, 99–101
Unix
    command line love, 194
    history, 23
    pushd and popd commands, 25
usefulness
    versus length, 10

V

Vasa ship wreck, 132
verification
    static analysis tools, 112
VI editor
    about, 179
    history, 24
views (see rooted views)
Virtual Desktop Manager (Windows), 50
virtual desktops, 48
virtual folders
    project management, 47
virtualization
    using, 80
Visual Studio
    search versus navigation, 33

W

web applications
    acceptance testing, 58

web sites
    automating interactions, 54
    mirroring, 53
    Selenium, 58
wget utility, 53
wikis
    Subversion example, 88
Windows, xiii
    (see also PowerToys; Virtual Desktop
    Manager)
    address bar, 20
    batch files, 61
    Command Prompt Explorer Bar, 26
    Cygwin, 192
    history, 23
    launchers, 11, 12
    rooted views, 44
Windows Power Shell, 61
workspace
    indirection, 73
    monitors, 48
    virtual desktops, 48

X

XML
    refactoring, 183

Y

YAGNI (You Ain't Gonna Need It), 130–133
Yahoo! Pipes, 54
yak shaving, 67

Z

zero-based arrays
    Java, 168

About the Author

Neal Ford a is software architect and Meme Wrangler at ThoughtWorks, a global IT consultancy with an exclusive focus on end-to-end software development and delivery. Before joining ThoughtWorks, Neal was the chief technology officer at The DSW Group, Ltd., a nationally recognized training and development firm. Neal has a degree in computer science, specializing in languages and compilers, from Georgia State University and a minor in mathematics, specializing in statistical analysis. He is also the designer and developer of applications, instructional materials, magazine articles, video presentations, and author of the books *Developing with Delphi: Object-Oriented Techniques* (Prentice-Hall), *JBuilder 3 Unleashed* (Sams), and *Art of Java Web Development* (Manning). He was editor of and contributor to the 2006 and 2007 editions of the *No Fluff, Just Stuff Anthology* (Pragmatic Bookshelf). His language proficiencies include Java, C#/.NET, Ruby, Groovy, functional languages, Scheme, Object Pascal, C++, and C. His primary consulting focus is the design and construction of large-scale enterprise applications. Neal has taught on-site classes nationally and internationally to the military and to many Fortune 500 companies. He is also an internationally acclaimed speaker, having spoken at over 100 developer conferences worldwide, delivering more than 600 talks. If you have an insatiable curiosity about Neal, visit his web site at *http://www.nealford.com*. He welcomes feedback and can be reached at *nford@thoughtworks.com*.

Colophon

The cover image is a stock photograph from Corbis. The text font is Adobe's Meridien; the heading font is ITC Bailey.